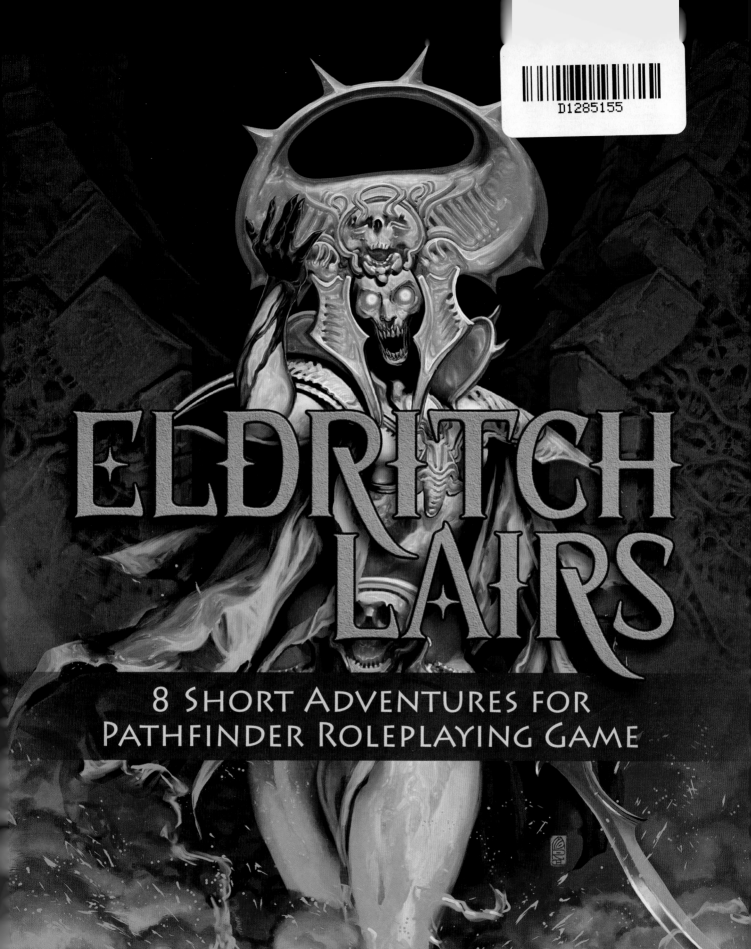

# ELDRITCH LAIRS

## 8 Short Adventures for Pathfinder Roleplaying Game

# ELDRITCH LAIRS

## CREDITS

**DESIGN:** James J. Haeck, Jerry LeNeave, Mike Shea, Bill Slavicsek

**PATHFINDER ROLEPLAYING GAME DESIGN:** Mike Welham

**COVER ART:** Marcel Mercado

**INTERIOR ART:** Marcel Mercado, Florian Stitz, Bryan Syme

**CARTOGRAPHY:** Jon Pintar, Michael Tumey

**EDITING:** Joe Pasini

**ART DIRECTION:** Marc Radle

**LAYOUT AND GRAPHIC DESIGN:** Marc Radle

**PUBLISHER:** Wolfgang Baur

KOBOLD PRESS
PO Box 2811
Kirkland WA 98083

www.koboldpress.com

# Table of Contents

## A NOTE ABOUT MONSTERS

If a creature cannot be found within the *Pathfinder Roleplaying Game* Reference Document (PRD), then either the creature's statistics or a reference to the *Midgard Bestiary* is provided.

# PIT OF THE DUST GOBLINS

An adventure for five 4th-level characters set in the Western Wastes

*by James J. Haeck*

## GM INTRODUCTION

Pit of the Dust Goblins is a trap-laden lair set at the edge of Midgard's Western Wastes in the ruins of the town of Feycircle. It is a short dungeon that requires stealth, clever tactics, and manipulation of different factions within the dungeon to ensure survival. This dungeon can be linked to the Crypt of Green Shadows and the Carrion Shrine of Qorgeth, but it can also be used as a stand-alone dungeon.

## SUMMARY

The people of Feycircle believed the fairy ring their town was named for protected them from the encroaching sands of the Western Wastes. When the ring withered, they learned they were right. Feycircle's dew-flecked pastures and verdant forests succumbed to the Wastes in an instant.

Feycircle is now sunken deep in the sands and occupied primarily by a tribe of fanatical dust goblins, a herd of dogmoles, and the giant worms that caused the blight. The PCs can explore the former town's keep—the only structure remaining in the dusty sinkhole now called the Pit of the Dust Goblins. Inside the keep is an entrenched gatekeeper who can divulge that two children remain in town, imprisoned by the goblins.

The dust goblins have summoned and imprisoned a selang—a shadow fey—inside the blighted fairy circle. The goblins fear open combat and have laced the sunken keep with traps, and they would sooner parley than fight.

### FACTIONS

The following groups and individuals play an important role in this adventure.

**Beasts.** The Pit is currently inhabited by two kinds of beasts: crusher worms and dogmoles. The crushers are the spawn of Qorgeth, Demon Lord of Worms. The worms and their dread master are the cause of the blight, and they live only to feed. Were it not for a wandering pack of worm-hunting dogmoles, they would have consumed Feycircle already. Escaped from a dwarven settlement, the domesticated dogmoles sought refuge and regular meals in the ruins of Feycircle. The dust goblins treat their unlikely allies with uncommon kindness.

**Dust Goblins.** The goblins squatting in the ruins of Feycircle are outcasts from the Bloody Tusks tribe, cultists exiled for venerating the mysterious shadow fey instead of the Great Old Ones that lumber across the Wastes. The leader of the goblins is a shaman named Sisskuss who leapt at the chance to capture the abandoned fairy ring, a nexus of power at the crossing of two minor ley lines. Sisskuss has summoned a shadow fey called a selang inside the circle, hoping to court it and empower her bloodline with its dark magic.

**Selang.** The selang is the goblins' unwilling captive, and he is willing to strike a bargain in exchange for their total annihilation. Like all fey, however, the selang's moods are fickle, and he is just as likely to cheat the PCs as he is to reward them.

**Survivors.** Three humans remain in the Pit of the Dust Goblins. The first is Hana, a loyal gatekeeper who has vowed to watch the town no matter what. She is trapped within her home, though she hopes to find two young siblings named Rennie and Linde who were unable to flee. She believes (correctly) that they are being held by the goblins as bargaining chips.

## ADVENTURE HOOKS

Most of the refugees from Feycircle have pitched tents some 20 miles from the city. As GM, you know best how to involve the PCs in this adventure. The following adventure hooks are provided to inspire and assist you.

- **Heroism.** Two children—a brother and sister named Rennie and Linde—are trapped inside the village. Their distraught mother, Relimma, is in the refugee camp, and she offers the PCs anything they want (up to the 50 gp she has to her name) in exchange for their safety. The siblings' father, Petring, ventured out to find them the day after the worms came, and hasn't been seen since.

- **Money.** Feycircle was not a poor village; the lord and lady lived comfortably in their keep, and a large amount of treasure is contained within. Greedy adventures may be lured by rumors of so much unattended wealth.

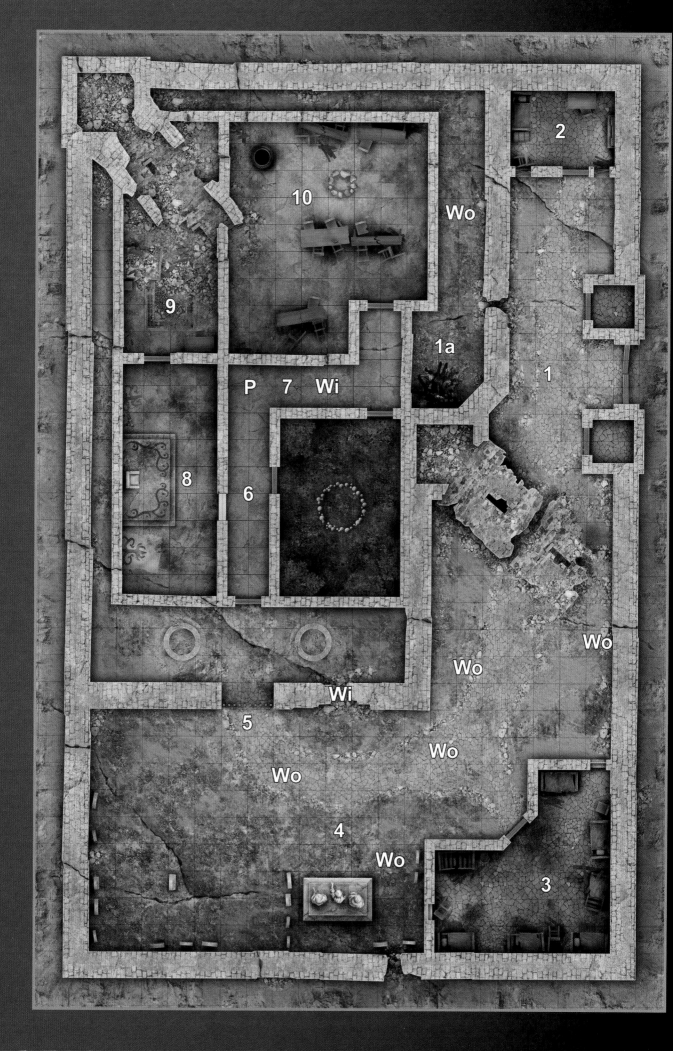

- **Protection.** The chief of the Bloody Tusks goblin tribe is disturbed by the success of Sisskuss and her fey-worshiping deviants and wants them wiped out. If the PCs seek safe travel across the Wastes, he is willing to offer protection on their journey if they destroy the exiled goblins.

# ADVENTURE START

*All that remains of Feycircle are a few shattered timbers protruding from the hungry sands, and they are joined by a dozen decaying corpses of goblins and man-sized worms. At the edge of the wreckage is a deep sinkhole—a vast pit that has devoured the town's keep. Its crumbling walls are still visible above the pit's edge. Looming on the horizon like a distant, black moon is the terrible silhouette of Anax Apogeion, one of the Great Old Ones that haunt the Western Wastes.*

## 1. MAIN GATE

*Thirty feet down the sandy slopes of the pit stand the slanted gates of Feycircle Keep. War cries and animal roars can be heard from within—just inside the walls of the keep, a battle has broken out! Goblins are hiding in a collapsed tower and shooting at gigantic lavender worms, and both sides seem preoccupied.*

A group of six dust goblins (see *Midgard Bestiary*, page 55) defend their turf against a swarm of eight giant crusher worms (use constrictor snake statistics). The goblins are barricaded within a fallen tower and raining crossbow bolts down on the worms. They see all intruders as enemies, but a PC succeeding at a DC 14 Diplomacy check can convince the goblins' boss, Tummy, to ally with the PCs out of necessity. Otherwise, if the PCs are spotted, two of the worms and half the goblins attack them immediately.

If the battle here goes south, a pair of dust goblins run to Area 3 to "release the hounds," adding four dogmoles (see *Midgard Bestiary*, page 35) to the fray.

**Collapsed Wall.** The sand pit that has devoured the keep has also destabilized the fortress's walls, and a small fissure has formed in the wall that lies just north of the gate. A character must succeed at a DC 18 Escape Artist check to slip through; failure by 5 or more means he takes 1d6 bludgeoning damage and does not enter. This fissure leads to Area 1a.

**Fallen Tower.** The tower is completely collapsed, but up to six Small creatures can squeeze inside, each of which must succeed at a DC 15 Escape Artist check as a standard action; a creature that fails by 5 or more takes 1d6 bludgeoning damage and does not enter. Creatures within the rubble have cover.

**Gate Towers.** The two 30-foot-tall watchtowers flanking the gate are still standing and relatively stable. They can both be ascended by climbing ladders (DC 5 Climb check) inside the walls.

**Worm Traps.** The dust goblins have spread worm traps all along the main road leading from the gate to the fortress. Each trap hides under the dust, snapping up with iron clamps when a Medium or larger creature steps on it.

| WORM TRAP | CR 1 |
|---|---|
| **Type** mechanical; **Perception** DC 15; **Disable Device** DC 20 | |

**EFFECTS**

**Trigger** location; **Reset** manual
**Effect** Atk +10 melee (2d6+3); creature is immobile and can escape with a DC 20 **Disable Device** check, DC 22 Escape Artist check, or DC 26 Strength check.

### 1A. DUSTY COURTYARD

*This narrow area with a collapsed wall to the south may once have been a beautiful flower garden, but the remaining flowers are now worm-eaten and withered. The stink of death hangs heavy in the eastern corner, where maggots swarm among a pile of human corpses.*

The milky-white death maggots devouring the bodies are the larval stage of the crusher worms infesting the sinkhole. A creature that investigates or otherwise disturbs a body must succeed at a DC 15 Reflex save or be immediately swarmed by these creatures. On a failed save, the maggots feed on the creature's flesh, inflicting 4d6 points of damage (DC 15 Fortitude save halves).

A character investigating the bodies can attempt a DC 13 Perception check. On a success, she finds valuables worth a total of 50 gp, including a rosewood holy symbol.

A small alley leads along the east end of the keep toward a room that has been crushed by a fallen tower. A character succeeding at a DC 14 Perception check notices that the interior of the castle is visible through the wreckage. A creature can attempt a DC 15 Escape Artist check to squeeze through; failure by 5 or more means that they take 1d6 bludgeoning damage and do not enter. This passage leads to the keep's bedroom (Area 9).

### 2. GATEKEEPER'S COTTAGE

*Just east of the main gate is a small cottage. Its bright yellow paint is faded and peeling, and the front window is boarded up. Its door bears the scars of recent assault.*

As soon as the PCs approach, they can each attempt a DC 10 Perception check. On a success, read the following.

*You approach the door and catch a glimpse of sudden movement behind the smashed window, which is covered only by planks of wood. You are just able to make out the tip of a crossbow bolt pointed through the boards—and aimed at you!*

Hana, Feycircle's loyal gatekeeper, was captured by the goblins when they took over, but she managed to escape. She's been trapped inside her house ever since, and the stress has made her paranoid. She wants to search for Rennie and Linde, the two missing children, but regular goblin patrols and dangerous worms make it impossible to leave.

Hana's home is sparsely decorated; she dismantled most of her furniture to build barricades and to board up the windows. She has a rack of four *potions of cure light wounds* hidden beneath her bed and an heirloom set of fine china worth 25 gp.

### What Hana Knows:

- The only other people who remained in town after the goblin attack were Rennie and Linde, their father, a butler named Petring, and a few now-deceased guards.
- The goblins have domesticated a herd of beasts called dogmoles and are using them to fight the worms.
- While she was the dust goblins' prisoner, she learned their leader is a shaman named Sisskuss, who has used the blighted fairy ring to summon a shadow fey.

| HANA | CR 1/2 |
|---|---|

**XP 200**
Female human fighter 1
NG Medium humanoid (human)
**Init** +2; **Senses** Perception +2

#### DEFENSE

**AC** 18, touch 12, flat-footed 16 (+6 armor, +2 Dex)
**hp** 13 (1d10+3)
**Fort** +4, **Ref** +2, **Will** +1

#### OFFENSE

**Speed** 20 ft.
**Melee** morningstar +3 (1d8+2)
**Ranged** mwk light crossbow +4 (1d8/19–20)

#### STATISTICS

**Str** 15, **Dex** 14, **Con** 14, **Int** 8, **Wis** 13, **Cha** 10
**Base Atk** +1; **CMB** +3; **CMD** 15
**Feats** Endurance, Point-Blank Shot, Precise Shot
**Skills** Perception +2, Sense Motive +2
**Languages** Common
**Combat Gear** *potion of cure light wounds*, alchemist's fire, tanglefoot bag; **Other Gear** chainmail, mwk light crossbow with 10 crossbow bolts, morningstar

### 3. SERVANTS' QUARTERS

*This house is filled with smashed bunks, overturned lavatory buckets, and splintered mops. Worm corpses are strewn around the room, and a pack of hound-sized beasts gnaws on the remains. The beasts' tentacled mouths eagerly slurp up wormflesh.*

The four worm-eating beasts are dogmoles (see *Midgard Bestiary*, page 35). They arrived in Feycircle a few days after the worms appeared. They are escaped domesticated beasts originally trained to track subterranean worms. The dust goblins found them easy to retrain and turn against the invading worms, and they use the servants' quarters as a kennel.

The dogmoles lash out if a creature gets too close, but a PC that succeeds at a DC 15 Handle Animal or wild empathy check can calm them. A character who makes three successful checks before three failures gains one of the beasts as an ally as if it were affected by the *charm animal* spell. It fights independently of its master.

### 4. CEMETERY

*Cracked gravestones lie strewn across a field of blackened grass. Bones jut awkwardly out of the sandy earth. A tentacled hound chews on a worm caught in an iron trap beside the only standing structure in the destroyed cemetery—a towering monument topped with the weathered statues of three knightly heroes.*

A dogmole is busy devouring the worm, but it is still famished. It attacks anything smelling of worm—including characters with worm blood on their clothes or weapons. The dust goblins at the gate in Area 5 might also

see characters in the cemetery and attack with their light crossbows. The gravestones in the cemetery provide partial cover to prone creatures.

**Collapsed Wall.** The goblins invaded by swarming through both the main gates and a collapsed portion of the wall behind the cemetery. It faces a shallow wall of the sinkhole and can be used to escape the keep by succeeding at a DC 10 Escape Artist check.

**Monument.** Amidst the smaller graves is a grand monument to three heroes: an elven paladin, a human wizard, and an elfmarked sorcerer. These warriors founded Feycircle and made a pact with the Summer Court. The fairy ring created by their pact has until recently kept the town safe from the Wastes. The answer to the magic's failure lies beneath this monument, in the Crypt of Green Shadows. A character succeeding at a DC 13 Perception check discovers that a slab bearing the heroes' names (Krythitas, Hassan, and Tymande Flamesong) can be moved. A staircase beneath leads into the crypt, but moving the slab causes three giant crusher worms (use constrictor snake statistics) to surge out of the opening.

## 5. PORTCULLIS AND COURTYARD

*Amid the keep's crumbling walls is a mighty iron portcullis. Five squat figures move about atop the battlements, crossbows drawn. To the south of the gate is a hole in the crumbling wall wide enough to pass through. On the eastern side is a granite fountain, now dry and full of sand.*

Five dust goblins stand atop the battlements above the gate and attack any humanoids or worms drawing near unless a truce has been made (such as with Tummy in Area 1). They can open the gate from the battlements, but a character that succeeds at a DC 25 Strength check can also force the portcullis open for 1 round.

**Collapsed Wall.** Part of the wall has crumbled just south of the gate, but it is heavily trapped. A trip wire hidden within the rubble drags a net barbed with poison hooks onto any creature that triggers it.

| BARBED NET TRAP | CR 4 |
|---|---|

**Type** mechanical; **Perception** DC 20; **Disable Device** DC 20

**EFFECTS**

**Trigger** location; **Reset** manual

**Effect** Atk +15 melee (2d6 piercing damage plus medium spider venom); creature is entangled in the net (which has 5 hp) and can escape with a successful DC 22 Escape Artist check or DC 25 Strength check (failure deals 1d6 piercing damage)

**Keep Courtyard.** Two beautiful fountains, now dry and full of sand, flank the door. There are heaps of money piled in the bottom of this fountain; if the PCs take 5 minutes to sift through each they recover a total of 40 gp in assorted coinage.

## 6. ENTRANCE HALLWAY

*The air inside the keep's entrance hall is dry and sour. The hall goes straight for thirty feet before turning to the right. There is a gold-embellished stone door on the north wall and a door carved from wood and decorated with an engraving of a crown of flowers on the south wall. The sweet smell of honey lingers around this door.*

The north door leads to the Audience Hall (Area 8) and the south door to the Shadow Ring (Area 11). At the eastern end of the hallway is a poorly concealed pit trap.

| PIT TRAP | CR 3 |
|---|---|

**Type** mechanical; **Perception** DC 10; **Disable Device** —

**EFFECTS**

**Trigger** location; **Reset** manual

**Bypass** DC 15 Acrobatics check to slip past the pit; failure by 5 or more causes a character to fall into the pit.

**Effect** 40-ft.-deep pit (4d6 falling damage); DC 20 Reflex avoids; multiple targets (all targets in a 10-ft.-square area)

## 7. SOUTHERN HALLWAY

*This hallway leads has one door to the west and one to the east, leading to the Shadow Ring (Area 11) and the Dining Hall (Area 10) respectively. The middle of this hallway is laced with dozens of nearly invisible strings, any of which can trigger a trap that causes numerous bone darts to shoot out from holes in the wall.*

| BONE DART TRAP | CR 4 |
|---|---|

**Type** mechanical; **Perception** DC 25; **Disable Device** 20

**EFFECTS**

**Trigger** location; **Reset** manual

**Effect** Atk +15 (4d6 piercing); multiple targets (all targets in a 10-ft.-square area)

## 8. AUDIENCE CHAMBER

*The walls of this wide chamber are covered in decaying tapestries of golden trees and crimson flowers. Against the back wall is a marble throne, and piled at its base are the eviscerated corpses of a dozen goblins. On the throne sits a bloody sword.*

The blood-coated sword is a +1 *dancing longsword* that has been magically bound to protect the throne from usurpers. If defeated in single combat, it acquiesces to its new master; however, until the wielder reaches 9th level, the sword can only use its *dancing* special ability once per day. If the sword is not defeated in a fair duel, it shatters when reduced to 0 hit points.

A short hallway in the east of the chamber leads to the Bedroom (Area 9).

## 9. BEDROOM

*A tower has fallen on this once-luxurious bedchamber. The splinters of a rich four-poster bed are strewn across the floor, mingling with scattered coins and the dust of pulverized flagstones. The collapsed tower has also smashed through part of the southern wall, and the smell of burning excrement as well as the sound of low, chittering voices emanate from beyond the wall.*

This room was once the lord and lady's bedroom. It has been smashed by a falling tower, creating a passage to the outside (see Area 1a). Similarly, the tower has crushed the south wall between here and the Dining Hall (Area 10). A character can make a DC 15 Escape Artist check to squeeze through; failure by 5 or more means she takes 1d6 damage and does not enter. Characters who want to clear the rubble can undergo 5 total work-hours of heavy labor to

clear a path, but the noise alerts the inhabitants of Area 10, who investigate by sneaking in via the Audience Chamber (Area 8).

Stones from the fallen tower have left debris of crushed armoires and bedside stands. A PC succeeding at a Perception check finds jewelry and coins worth a number of gold pieces equal to the result of the check × 10 gp; the check can be repeated but yields a maximum of only 500 gp. The jewelry includes sapphire earrings and a golden heart locket.

## 10. DINING HALL

*The culinary disaster being perpetrated in the dining hall smells like burning refuse. The body of a giant worm is turning on a spit, and several dust goblins dance gleefully around the flames, screeching cooking songs. A totem-draped shaman sits removed from the rest, meditating. A giant black stewpot is in the northeast corner, and muffled voices echo from within the pot.*

The dining hall is where Sisskuss, a dust goblin druid, and her main force of 8 dust goblins (see *Midgard Bestiary*, page 55) have made camp. The room is filled with upturned tables and chairs, and the goblins are busily figuring out how to roast worm meat, while Sisskuss is deep in meditation. Stealthy PCs may be able to save the children, Rennie and Linde, without alerting the goblins to their presence.

**Sisskuss and the Selang.** Sisskuss wants to mate with the selang to mix her bloodline with his dark power. If she is defeated, she realizes that her dream is dead and surrenders. She grudgingly offers to release the fey from the circle (see Area 11, Dismissing the Selang) if the characters agree to allow her and the goblins to continue living in the keep.

**Children.** The missing children, the precocious six-year-old Rennie and steely 10-year-old Linde, are tied up and sitting in a black iron stewpot in the northeast corner of the dining hall. It is full of water, and the goblins are making preparations to boil them alive if their worm feast doesn't pan out.

### What the Children Know:

- Linde saw her father in town just before she and her brother were captured by the goblins! He disappeared into a hole under the "big statues" in the cemetery.
- Linde knows where all the traps in town are, and will help the PCs avoid them.
- Rennie says that he and Linde first snuck into the castle through a hole made by the fallen tower (Area 9) and that they could escape the same way.

## SISSKUSS · CR 3

**XP 800**

Female advanced dust goblin druid 2

NE Small humanoid (goblinoid)

**Init** +4; **Senses** darkvision 60 ft.; Perception +7

### DEFENSE

**AC** 22, touch 15, flat-footed 18 (+4 armor, +4 Dex, +3 natural, +1 size)

**hp** 18 (2d8+6)

**Fort** +5, **Ref** +4, **Will** +5

**Weaknesses** light sensitivity

### OFFENSE

**Speed** 20 ft.

**Melee** mwk dagger +5 (1d2+1/19–20)

**Domain Spell-Like Abilities** (CL 2nd; concentration +4)

5/day—fire bolt (1d6+1 fire)

**Druid Spells Prepared** (CL 2nd; concentration +4)

1st—burning hands^D (DC 13), entangle (DC 13), longstrider, obscuring mist

0 (at will)—detect magic, puff of smoke^DM (DC 12), resistance, thunderclap^DM

^D **Domain** spell; **Domain** Fire (Ash^APG subdomain)

### STATISTICS

**Str** 12, **Dex** 18, **Con** 14, **Int** 14, **Wis** 14, **Cha** 12

**Base Atk** +1; **CMB** +1; **CMD** 15

**Feats** Weapon Finesse

**Skills** Climb +3, Handle Animal +6, Knowledge (nature) +9, Perception +7, Stealth +10, Survival +13; **Racial Modifiers** +4 Survival

**Languages** Aklo, Common, Druidic, Giant, Goblin

**SQ** fast, nature sense, twisted, wild empathy +3, woodland stride

**Combat Gear** potion of cure moderate wounds; **Other Gear** hide armor, mwk dagger, amulet of natural armor +1

### 11. SHADOW RING

*Shadow engulfs you as soon as open the door to this room. It spills from within like a mist rolling in from the sea, and it's impossible to see through the coiling shadows.*

Neither light nor darkvision can penetrate the darkness in this room (see Magical Darkness, below), though it is full of life despite the blight upon Feycircle. The air is hot and humid, and jet-black flowers bloom from vines climbing the walls and creeping across the floor. The room smells of honey and chocolate. Trapped inside a fairy ring is an indistinct humanoid silhouette.

**Magical Darkness.** Only characters that can see in magical darkness can see within this room, which is treated as if *deeper darkness* had been cast in it. A *daylight* (or more powerful) spell can dispel the darkness as per usual, but it does not dispel the shadows spilling forth from the corrupted fairy ring.

**Selang.** The fey trapped in the ring is a dark satyr known as a selang (see *Dark Fey*, page 8). He lives for slaughter and chaos, but he was trapped in this ring by Sisskuss and must do her bidding while he remains there. He wants vengeance against the goblins and promises to slaughter them all if the party breaks the ring and frees him.

**Breaking the Ring.** The selang is true to his word and helps the PCs slaughter the goblins, but he will turn on them afterward if he thinks he can overpower them. Freeing the selang by breaking the fairy ring seals Feycircle's fate; the Wastes can never be forced back without its power.

**Dismissing the Selang.** If the PCs defeated Sisskuss, she agrees to dismiss the selang, but she does not reveal that they will have to kill him. Her dismissal ritual allows the dark satyr to leave the fairy ring without the ring being broken. As soon as the selang is free, Sisskuss flees, hoping to escape in the confusion and return another day.

## SELANG · CR 6

**XP 2,400**

CE Medium fey (outsider)

**Init** +2; **Senses** darkvision 60 ft., low-light vision; Perception +17

### DEFENSE

**AC** 19, touch 13, flat-footed 16 (+2 Dex, +1 dodge, +6 natural)

**hp** 76 (8d10+32)

**Fort** +6, **Ref** +8, **Will** +8

**DR** 5/cold iron or magic; **Immune** acid, electricity

### OFFENSE

**Speed** 40 ft.

**Melee** dagger +12 (1d4+4/19–20 plus poison)

**Ranged** shortbow +10 (1d6/x3 plus poison)

**Special Attacks** alien piping, sleep poison

**Spell-Like Abilities** (CL 7th; concentration +11)

At will—dancing lights, ghost sound (DC 14)

3/day—fear (DC 18), beast shape II, sleep (DC 15), suggestion (DC 17)

### STATISTICS

**Str** 18, **Dex** 15, **Con** 18, **Int** 12, **Wis** 14, **Cha** 19

**Base Atk** +8; **CMB** +12; **CMD** 24

**Feats** Dodge, Iron Will, Mobility, Weapon Finesse

**Skills** Bluff +15, Diplomacy +11, Intimidate +15, Knowledge (planes) +8, Perception +17, Perform (wind instruments) +15, Sense Motive +13, Stealth +13, Survival +13; **Racial Modifiers** +4 Perception, +4 Perform (wind instruments), +4 Survival

**Languages** Aklo, Sylvan, Trade Tongue

### SPECIAL ABILITIES

**Alien Piping (Su)** A selang can confuse and injure his enemies by playing weird, ear-bending harmonies on his alien pipes, made from the beaks, cartilage, and throat sacs of a dorreq. When the dark satyr plays a tune on his pipes, all creatures within a 60 ft. radius must succeed at a DC 18 Will save or be affected by *confusion, contagion, hideous laughter, irresistible dance,* or *mass charm monster,* depending on what alien and otherworldly music the selang chooses to play. A creature that successfully saves against this sonic mind-affecting effect cannot be affected by the piping for 24 hours, but it is still subject to attack by the selang's other spell-like abilities. The dark satyr can use each of the above spell-like effects once per day. The save DC is Charisma-based.

**Sleep Poison (Ex)** Selangs coat their weapons with a sleep poison made from the brain fluids of dorreqi, and any creature injured by a coated weapon must succeed at a DC 18 Fortitude save or fall asleep for 2d6 rounds. The save DC is Constitution-based.

## CONCLUSION

If you are running this dungeon as a stand-alone adventure, defeating the selang and purifying the fairy ring sees life return to Feycircle. The worms flee and new blades of grass begin to poke through the newly invigorated soil. Rennie and Linde can be returned to their mother, though their father might never be seen again. Depending on how Sisskuss and the goblins were dealt with, Feycircle may once again be a prosperous village—one where the PCs have many new friends.

If you plan on connecting this dungeon to the Crypt of Green Shadows and the Carrion Shrine of Qorgeth, then the PCs are not so lucky. Feycircle remains fallow until the taint of Qorgeth is eradicated.

**Continuing the Adventure.** Petring's children saw their father disappear into a hole beneath the Heroes' Monument in the town graveyard. The PCs learn that Feycircle's desolation is due to Petring foolishly invoking the power of Qorgeth, Demon Lord of Worms, and creating a shrine to his dark master beneath the crypts.

# CRYPT OF GREEN SHADOWS

An adventure for five 5th-level characters set in the Western Wastes

*by James J. Haeck*

## GM INTRODUCTION

The Lord of Worms will consume all, and his feast begins in the Crypt of Green Shadows. Wormhearted invaders have breached the walls of the labyrinthine mausoleum, and their mere presence sows chaos and madness among the dead. The crypt was once the resting place of three heroes who forged peace between humans and the Unseelie fey, but the gnawing mouths of Qorgeth's worms have ended the heroes' peaceful slumber. This unholy incursion has drawn the wrath of both the spirits of the dead and the shadow fey who created the crypt.

## SUMMARY

This dungeon can be used to continue the adventure in the Pit of the Dust Goblins or as a stand-alone adventure. The children Rennie and Linde from the previous adventure are in search of their father, Petring, who they saw disappear into the crypts beneath town.

The crypt is thick with supernatural shadow. Torches can be lit from a brazier of green faerie fire, which cuts through magical darkness, in the entrance. The torches burn rapidly, and the PCs must travel quickly to preserve their light until they reach the funeral pyre in the heart of the crypt. There they can learn the way to the Carrion Shrine of Qorgeth.

## FACTIONS

The following groups and individuals play an important role in this adventure.

**Heroic Spirits.** The city of Feycircle above the crypt was founded on a truce made between three knightly heroes and the courts of the shadow fey. These heroes are Krythitas, an elven paladin, Hassan, a human wizard, and Tymande Firestorm, an elfmarked sorcerer. Qorgeth's worms have started to devour their bodies, sending their spirits into a murderous rage.

**Shadow Fey.** The three heroes shared an unbreakable bond with the Queen of the Shadow Fey. When the heroes passed, her servants created a tomb that would protect the heroes' bodies and riches for all time. When the worms invaded this sanctuary, the heroes' spirits called out for protection; a number of shadow fey warriors have answered the call, but they are cornered in Area 6.

**Spawn of Qorgeth.** Qorgeth's servants blindly consume everything they can find. Only creatures who pledge their devotion to the Writhing Prince himself are spared their hunger. In addition to the mindless worms, Petring's foul rituals have called several wormhearted suffragans to his cause. They care little for why Petring summoned them; they are far more interested in claiming the arcane relics entombed here in the name of their dark lord and letting their worms devour the rest.

## ADVENTURE HOOKS

As GM, you know best how to involve the PCs in this adventure. The following adventure hooks are provided to inspire and assist you.

- **Contact**. As part of an ongoing campaign, the PCs must contact the spirits of a legendary hero or group of heroes. Krythitas, Hassan, and Tymande can be used as is, or you can replace them with heroes suitable for your campaign. Their spirits must be pacified before they can be contacted.

- **Magic**. The heroic wizard Hassan was entombed with his spellbook. Its pages are rumored to contain countless spells of unimaginable power. The wormhearted servants of Qorgeth seek its power too and are overjoyed to slaughter any competition.

- **Unfinished Business**. Following the adventure in the Pit of the Dust Goblins, the children Rennie and Linde direct the PCs to the heroes' crypt in search of their father, Petring. Petring is in over his head and is now a prisoner within the Carrion Shrine of Qorgeth, deep below the crypt. The path to the shrine is hidden in the twisting passages of Area 3.

## ADVENTURE START

The PCs enter the crypt by descending two flights of perfectly smooth stone stairs. Petring's footprints are visible in the dust. As they near the bottom of the stairs, they are engulfed by a haze of eerie, green shadows.

**Green Shadows.** Shadow envelops the entire dungeon. It is a form of magical darkness; light does not penetrate it and creatures with darkvision cannot see through it. Spectral, humanoid forms seem to move through the shadows when viewed from a distance, and unintelligible whispering can be heard within the haze. The shadows also create a permanent *gentle repose* effect within the crypt.

**Navigating the Crypt.** Effects that penetrate magical darkness still work within the green shadows but have their range and duration halved. Torches, candles, and lanterns can be lit from the brazier of green faerie fire in Area 1, but they shed magical light in half their usual radius. Most importantly, light sources lit from this flame burn out after 1 minute and can be extinguished by strong wind. Because of this, tracking time is especially important in this dungeon. As each round is 6 seconds, the GM can easily track time in the dungeon by using a d10 to count up each round until 1 minute has passed.

## 1. HALL OF GREEN FLAMES

*A set of stairs lead into a circular chamber that is illuminated by a brazier of green flames in the center of the floor. Three stone doors carved with delicate floral sigils impede passage to the north, west, and east. The air is dry and stale.*

The green flames dispel magical darkness. The brass brazier holding the inextinguishable fire in this room can be moved, but the flame does not move with it, instead remaining suspended a foot above the ground.

**Doors.** The doors leading out of this room are covered in flowery fey designs and Sylvan script. The north door reads "Krythitas watches the Funeral Pyre," the west door reads "Hassan watches the Hall of Secrets," and the east door reads "Tymande watches the Pit of Undying Fire."

## 2. HALL OF HOWLING SPIRITS

*Wails of agony pierce your ears when you open the door. An icy wind strikes like a charging bull and the air is knocked from your lungs. Suddenly, the room is plunged into darkness as the wind extinguishes all flame!*

The first time the PCs enter this room, their light is extinguished without a save. In the future, they may make a DC 10 Reflex save to protect their light. The howling spirits in this hallway are loud but otherwise harmless.

**Corpse.** In the middle of this hall is the corpse of a shadow fey guardian from Area 7. Its muscular body is 10 feet long and covered in maggots.

## 3. HALL OF SECRETS

*A labyrinthine hallway is filled with swirling green shadows. Somewhere in the maze of small twisting passages, someone is humming a quiet tune: "Hum hum, by my green candle…"*

A wraith and two shadows drift counterclockwise around the main loop of this area. The wraith is the deranged spirit of the human wizard Hassan and carries a green candlestick in a cracked porcelain teapot. The eerie glow casts light in only a 5-foot radius, and the wraith does not notice any creatures outside its light. Hassan's spectral figure appears similar to his physical body in Area 5; his thick black beard is braided into dozens of tiny strands, and his magnificent robes billow around him as if blown by a wild wind.

**Hassan.** The wizard's spirit patrols these corridors and attacks all non-fey on sight, though he can only see creatures adjacent to him. He uses a *candle of daylight* to illuminate the area around him, allowing his shadow retainers to see his enemies as well. This spirit can be dispelled by reducing it to 0 hit points, extinguishing the candle, or immolating Hassan's physical body on the funeral pyre (see Area 12). Hassan cannot be reasoned with unless the PCs present one of Hassan's companions' treasured artifacts. If this is done, he regains his senses for 1 minute and urges the PCs to seek Krythitas in the northernmost room for a way to set the heroes' spirits to rest.

**Candle of Daylight.** Though Hassan is incorporeal, the candle is a solid object and can be handled by living and dead creatures. This *candle of daylight* sheds green light in a 5-foot radius when lit. By speaking "Candle, reveal all things!" a wielder can cause the light to surge outward, casting light in a 60-foot radius for 1 hour as the *daylight* spell. This ability cannot be used again until after the next dawn.

**Secrets.** This area has two secret doors; both are marked by a carving of Hassan putting his finger to his lips. A character that succeeds at a DC 15 Sense Motive or DC 20 Perception check learns how to open the door by mimicking Hassan's gesture and "shushing" the wall. The southeastern passage leads to Area 10 and emerges into an empty sarcophagus. The northwestern passage leads to a staircase that descends into the Carrion Shrine of Qorgeth.

**Trapped and Locked Doors.** Two doors in the north lead to Hassan's reliquary and burial chamber, Areas 4 and 5. The door to 4 displays an image of Hassan calling fire down from the sky.

| FLAME STRIKE TRAP | CR 6 |
|---|---|

**Type** magic; **Perception** DC 30; **Disable Device** DC 30

**EFFECTS**

**Trigger** proximity (alarm); **Reset** none

**Effect** spell effect (*flame strike*, 8d6 fire damage, half of which cannot be reduced by resistance or immunity, DC 17 Reflex save for half damage); multiple targets (all targets in a 10-ft.-radius cylinder)

The locked door to Area 5 requires a DC 20 Disable Device check to unlock and bears an image of Hassan sleeping on a stone slab.

## 4. HASSAN'S RELIQUARY

*This chamber is divided by a stone wall, in the center of which is a glowing barrier. Within the barrier is a tome upon a pedestal. Shining treasure is strewn across the floor, but from beyond the partition you can hear the sounds of steel striking stone.*

The wizard Hassan had his tomb separated in three: one portion for the arcane relics he had collected throughout his life, one portion for his body, and a small alcove in the center for his spellbook.

**Treasure.** The reliquary is filled with mundane treasure, such as gold and platinum coins, and gem-encrusted ceremonial weapons worth a total of 3,000 gp. If your campaign substitutes a legendary hero for Hassan, this reliquary may have a signature legendary item in it; otherwise the treasure chamber also contains a *brooch of shielding* and an *eagle cape*UE.

**Spellbook.** Hassan's spellbook is on a pedestal in the center of his burial chamber. It is surrounded by a permanent translucent barrier that functions as an antilife shell. This barrier can be temporarily dispelled using dispel magic or similar spells (and returns after 1 minute), but PCs can use other ingenious methods to obtain the spellbook, since nonliving matter passes through the barrier without resistance. The spellbook contains up to 70 levels of spells, or the following spells at the indicated levels:

> 1st – *burning hands, identify, mage armor, magic missile, shield*
> 2nd – *acid arrow, darkvision, knock, levitate, rope trick*
> 3rd – *fireball, gentle repose, haste, magic circle against evil, slow, vampiric touch, water breathing*
> 4th – *black tentacles, dimension door, secure shelter, stoneskin*
> 5th – *hold monster, passwall, polymorph*

## 5. HASSAN'S TOMB

*This chamber is divided by a stone wall, in the center of which is a glowing barrier. Within the barrier is a tome upon a pedestal. The chamber is spattered with dark blood, and three armored warriors are mechanically hacking at six man-sized worms struggling to get inside a stone sarcophagus.*

Three suits of animated armor tasked with defending Hassan's body are beset by six giant worms (use constrictor snake statistics), and the corpses of a dozen more worms are strewn across the room. The suits of armor attack all creatures who touch Hassan's perfectly preserved body.

**Secret.** In the northeast corner of the room is a statue of Hassan looking heroic. A character that succeeds at a DC 19 Perception check notices a groove in the floor, allowing the statue to be pulled 1 foot west. Moving the statue in this way opens a secret door to Area 12.

| ANIMATED ARMOR | CR 4 |
|---|---|

**XP 1,200**
**Animated object**
N Medium construct
**Init** +0; **Senses** darkvision 60 ft., low-light vision; Perception -5

**DEFENSE**

**AC** 16, touch 10, flat-footed 16 (+6 natural)
**hp** 36 (3d10+20)
**Fort** +1, **Ref** +1, **Will** −4
**Defensive Abilities** hardness 10; **Immune** construct traits

**OFFENSE**

**Speed** 30 ft.
**Melee** 2 slams +5 (1d8+2)

**STATISTICS**

**Str** 14, **Dex** 10, **Con** —, **Int** —, **Wis** 1, **Cha** 1
**Base Atk** +3; **CMB** +5; **CMD** 15
**SQ** construction points (4, additional attack, improved attack, metal)

## 6. INSIDE THE WORM

*Instead of a door at the end of this hallway, there is the toothy maw of a gargantuan purple worm! Faint slurping sounds echo from inside its gullet.*

The purple worm that devoured this hallway died 1 day ago, slain by the shadow fey in Area 7. Its gullet is still wet. Three young purple worms (use constrictor snake statistics and apply the giant creature template) are inside its body, devouring it from within, but they are hungry for even fresher flesh.

**Fey Door.** The shadow fey have created a magical gateway between the inside of the purple worm and their base in Area 7. Its onyx-black archway glistens with amethyst light, and the other chamber can be seen clearly through it.

## 7. SHADOW FEY CAMP

*This tomb has been converted into a military camp. Two ten-foot-tall, hulking creatures with gray-black skin and glimmering chain shirts stand arguing around an unlit brass brazier. Despite their monstrous size, their speech sounds elven.*

The shadow fey arrived to protect the heroes a few days ago. They were originally led by an enchantress named Xarrika, but she was ambushed by the wormhearted suffragan in Area 8 and hurled into the Pit of Undying Flame. Now all that remains is the muscle; two dumb, hulking giant shadow fey (see *Midgard Bestiary*, page 85, and apply the giant creature template). They are lost without Xarrika's leadership and are bickering in their camp about the best course of action to protect their heroes. A PC can attempt a DC 19 Diplomacy check to convince them to go along with any reasonable plan.

**Brazier.** The shadow fey can see up to 60 feet in magical darkness and have left the brass brazier unlit. It is filled with tinder and can be lit with green flame from the entrance to create another inextinguishable source of flame.

**Sarcophagi.** Four sarcophagi are arranged along the western wall of this room. Inside are the corpses of Tymande's retainers, perfectly preserved by the gentle repose effect that pervades the crypt. Searching the sarcophagi yields a *+1 dagger*, a mithral chain shirt, a silk burial shroud worth 50 gp, and 52 gp.

**Secret.** A section of wall in the northwest corner has a picture of the the elfmarked sorcerer Tymande Firestorm with daggers crossed in front of her chest. The wall slides open if a character adopts the same pose in front of it (something a PC can learn with a successful DC 20 Knowledge [local] check), leading to the inside of an empty sarcophagus in Area 10.

## 8. PIT OF UNDYING FLAME

*Two marble platforms, one in the north and one in the south, sit above a sea of fire and are connected by a narrow stone bridge. A cowled figure wheezes and rises to its feet on the platform on the north end of the room. Humanoid shapes move within the flames.*

The floor of this chamber is a sea of emerald fire. All entrances to this room are on elevated stone platforms 10 feet above the flames. A 3-foot-wide stone bridge connects north and south platforms. Meditating on the north platform is a wormhearted suffragan that awakens as soon as the PCs enter. It casts *command* on the first PC it sees, pointing a gnarled finger and rasping "Approach." The PC must move toward it by the shortest and most direct route, ending its turn if it moves within 5 feet of the suffragan.

Within the pit are 6 flaming skeletons. They climb up the platforms to attack the PCs in melee. They are skeletons with the fire subtype, they have a 5-foot fiery aura (1d6 fire), and their melee attacks deal an additional 1d6 points of fire damage. They are CR 1 creatures.

| WORMHEARTED SUFFRAGAN | CR 4 |
| --- | --- |

**XP 1,200**

CE Medium undead

**Init** +7; **Senses** darkvision 60 ft.; Perception +11

### DEFENSE

**AC** 17, touch 13, flat-footed 14 (+3 Dex, +4 natural)

**hp** 37 (5d8+15)

**Fort** +4, **Ref** +4, **Will** +7

**Immune** undead traits

**Weaknesses** vulnerability to positive energy

### OFFENSE

**Speed** 30 ft.

**Melee** 2 slams +6 (2d6 plus disease)

**Special Attacks** disease

**Spell-Like Abilities** (CL 5th; concentration +8)

At will—*command* (DC 14), *detect good*

3/day—*inflict moderate wounds* (DC 15)

1/day—*animate dead, blindness/deafness* (DC 16), *hold person* (DC 15), *speak with dead* (DC 16)

### STATISTICS

**Str** 10, **Dex** 17, **Con** —, **Int** 11, **Wis** 16, **Cha** 17

**Base Atk** +3; **CMB** +3; **CMD** 16

**Feats** Combat Casting, Improved Initiative, Weapon Finesse

**Skills** Heal +8, Intimidate +11, Knowledge (religion) +8, Perception +11

### SPECIAL ABILITIES

**Disease (Ex)** *Helminth Infestation*: Slam—injury; *save* Fort DC 15; *onset* 1 day; *frequency* 1 day; *effect* 1d4 Con and victim cannot regain hit points through rest; *cure* 2 consecutive saves.

## 9. TYMANDE'S TOMB

*This sepulcher reverberates with unearthly screams as the wraith of a husky elfmarked plunges its daggers into the cloaked figure before it. No blood spills from the wound as the figure turns to face you. Through rotting lips, it growls, "Hurry. Together, we can destroy this spirit."*

Tymande's spirit watches over her lifeless body— interred in a sarcophagus in the tomb's northeast corner— as a wraith. She is locked in combat with a wormhearted suffragan and four giant worms (use constrictor snake statistics) seeking to devour her corpse. The suffragan sees the PCs as potential allies and offers them wealth or information in exchange for their aid in destroying Tymande. It honors its agreement until the PCs have let their guard down.

**Tymande.** Tymande's spirit is mad with rage and cannot be reasoned with unless the PCs present one of her companions' treasured artifacts. If this is done, she regains her senses for 1 minute and urges the PCs to seek Krythitas in the northernmost room for a way to set the heroes' spirits to rest.

**Treasure.** Tymande was a Pact of the Blade sorcerer in service of the Great Old Ones wandering Midgard's Western Wastes. Her pact weapon was the *dagger of venom* now laid across her chest. She wears a set of *+1 glamered studded leather* enchanted to look like a flowing robe with a flame-embroidered collar.

**Secret.** A heroic statue of Tymande stands against the west wall. A character succeeding on a DC 19 Perception check notices a groove in the floor allowing the statue to be pulled 1 foot east. Moving the statue in this way opens a secret door in the wall to Areas 3 and 7.

## 10. RETAINERS' TOMB

*This hallway is flanked by ten upright sarcophagi. For a tomb, the room smells surprisingly fresh, as if there were no dead interred here.*

This hallway is home to the sarcophagi of eight of the three heroes' loyal soldiers. The wormhearted suffragan in Area 8 transformed these warriors into zombies. The zombies throw the lids off their sarcophagi as soon as the PCs fully enter the hall. Nothing physically indicates these perfectly preserved warriors are undead other than their glowing red eyes.

**Secret.** The two central coffins on the east and west of the hall do not have zombies inside. If they are opened, a wall with the carved image of a hero is revealed. See Areas 3 and 6 for their descriptions.

**Trap.** When the northern door is opened, a trap door in the floor in front of the door falls open.

| SURPRISE TRAP DOOR TRAP | CR 5 |
|---|---|

**Type** mechanical; **Perception** DC 23; **Disable Device** 28

**EFFECTS**

**Trigger** location; **Reset** manual

**Effect** 20-ft.-deep pit (2d6 falling damage); DC 23 Reflex avoids; multiple targets (all targets in a 10-ft. square area)

## 11. DRAINAGE DITCH

The green light pervading the crypt makes the river of crimson blood in this ditch appear to be made up of a sticky black ichor. The perfectly preserved corpses of would-be tomb raiders lie broken and mangled beneath the trap door. The blood of the giant worm slaughtered in Area 12 drains through an iron grate into this ditch. A door to the east carved with spiraling flame sigils leads to Area 8.

## 12. FUNERAL PYRE

*This room is clearly the heart of the crypt. In the room's center is a slab of white marble that shines like moonlight in the darkness. It has a slight indent, wide enough to hold three people side-by-side, that serves a shallow basin filled with dry cedar, frankincense, and rosemary. A single door stands behind the bloody corpse of a giant, milky-white worm.*

**The Pyre.** The shadow fey that built this crypt feared that evil might one day seek the hidden crypt to corrupt its tenants, even in death. As a safeguard, they constructed a funeral pyre with which to purify their spirits by immolating the bodies of the three heroes. The sacred herbs filling the pyre and the Sylvan runes carved around its edge help give peace to their restless souls. Only igniting the pyre with green flame from Area 1, Area 8, or Hassan's green candle (from Area 3) will complete the ritual.

**Completing the Ritual.** Cremating the bodies of the heroes abates their rage, and their spirits (regardless of whether their wraiths were defeated) appear above the flickering pyre. See "Conclusion" for how the spirits thank the PCs.

**Secrets.** Two secret doors open into this room from Areas 5 and 9. They cannot be opened from this side.

## 13. KRYTHITAS'S TOMB

*Two rows of decorative columns line this hall, which disappears into shadowy darkness beyond the light of your flame. The floor and pillars of the hall are spattered with black blood, and the bisected corpses of dozens of worms litter the floor.*

A character who succeeds at a DC 26 Perception check when entering the room notices a silhouetted figure hiding behind one of the pillars closest to the door. This figure is Krythitas, now an advanced wight wearing half-plate armor (increasing its AC to 23 and its flat-footed AC to 22)

and armed with a *+1 longsword* and *+1 longbow*. Krythitas remains some of her mind and sense of holy purpose, but only freeing her wrathful spirit (see Area 12) will restore her senses.

At the far end of this room is Krythitas' sarcophagus, its lid thrown on the floor. Piled in front of it are the corpses of a wormhearted suffragan and two shadow fey guardians. Nothing is inside the sarcophagus. Krythitas strikes when the PCs examine the sarcophagus.

Krythitas initially attacks with her longbow and cannot be reasoned with unless the PCs present one of her companions' treasured artifacts. If this is done, Krythitas momentarily regains her senses. She realizes that the heroes' spirits have been driven into a rage by Qorgeth's minions, and she tells the PCs that the only way to end their wrath is to cremate their corpses on the pyre in Area 12 using green flame. She remains lucid for only 1 minute, after which she continues attacking anyone in sight.

# CONCLUSION

If you are running this dungeon as a stand-alone adventure, defeating the minions of Qorgeth and absconding with the treasure may be enough for treasure-hunting heroes. However, cremating the corpses of Krythitas, Hassan, and Tymande grants an additional reward. When their bodies are consumed by the purifying flames, their spirits rise above the pyre and thank the PCs for setting them free from Qorgeth's madness. They offer a choice of reward:

**Information.** If the PCs are seeking Petring and the Carrion Shrine of Qorgeth, Hassan directs the PCs to the hidden stairs in Area 3 leading to it. Otherwise, the spirits offer one deep secret from the campaign world.

**Power.** The spirits offer to improve one relic of the PCs' choice; Hassan transforms the candle of daylight into a candle of invocation, Tymande increases the *dagger of venom's* save DC to 17, or Krythitas transforms one of her *+1 weapons* into a *+1 vicious weapon*.

**Continuing the Adventure.** Petring has lost control of the demonic forces he summoned. He invoked Qorgeth's power with the best of intentions, hoping to protect his home, but brought only ruin upon it and himself. He is now a prisoner in the Carrion Shrine of Qorgeth and will soon be consumed by his dark master.

# UNDER THE DEVIL'S THUMB

An adventure for five 5th-level characters set in the Southlands

*by Jerry LeNeave*

## GM INTRODUCTION

Under the Devil's Thumb is an adventure of choices, double crosses, and devious puzzles that tests the capabilities of even the most able adventurers.

## HISTORY & BACKGROUND

Nakresh, the eight-armed simian demon-god of thieves and unscrupulous wizards, is alive and well in the Southlands. The fingers of his lowermost left hand are represented by five individuals known as The Exalted. These five cultists are extremely cunning and audacious, and they are the most devoted to Nakresh. Such dedication means they perpetrate some of the highest crimes, heists, and robberies in known history.

Currently the five Exalted are: Lord Vermin, a male roachling rogue; Master Kiprak, a male kobold alchemist; Mognyr Dunestalker, a female gnoll ranger; Sister Starkfeather, a female ravenfolk cleric; and Zheita the Magicmonger, a female derro sorceress.

Every eight years the Exalted partake in their most grandiose crimes, even scheming against one another in an effort to prove who is the most pious servant of Nakresh. The outcome of this competition is determined by the monetary value of all the spoils of these heists, and a secret ballot is cast by lesser cult members. Of course, the Exalted may not kill one another or turn one another over to authorities.

The winner is given the rank of "Venerated Exalted" and holds the title for the next eight years. Should one of the Exalted seats become vacant—either by death, expulsion, or capture without hope of rescue—the other four vote to raise a 5th member to fill the seat from among the capable thieves of the region.

### SISTER STARKFEATHER

*Under the Devil's Thumb* focuses primarily on two of the five Exalted: Sister Starkfeather and Lord Vermin. Sister Starkfeather, an albino ravenfolk cleric, is the current Venerated Exalted of the lower left hand of Nakresh, and she plans to hold that position until she dies of old age. Her eight-year reign is set to end in just a few months, and Sister Starkfeather is already beginning to take steps to ensure her victory over her fiercest competitor, Lord Vermin.

### LORD VERMIN

Lord Vermin, an ambitious roachling rogue who happens to be the newest of the five Exalted, claims ownership of many subterranean lairs under the city of Highgate, as well as all of its appointed officials. He is eager to win the next contest, and his devotees, known as the Umbers, are anxious to assist. Ever aware of his people's relatively short lifespan, he is determined to win the contest, as it may be the last chance he gets in his lifetime.

### HIGHGATE

South of Per-Xor and just off the Lotus Trail, resting on the east bank of the River Nuria, sits the city of Highgate. This bastion of high-walled white limestone stands in stark contrast to the low rolling sands of the surrounding desert.

Built hundreds of years ago to serve as a defensive station during darker times, before the taming of the gnolls, Highgate is just as formidable now as it was then. An engineering marvel, even for something built so long ago, Highgate is an advanced city. Resting on the River Nuria allows it to have aqueducts and a fully functioning sewer system.

Inside, though, the city is anything but gleaming. It is overcome with a sickness of unknown origin—one that is being exploited to keep its people obedient through fear. Once ruled by pharaohs and sultans, Highgate now rests on the backs of the meek—corrupt "elected" officials who take bribes for silence and turn a blind eye to crime. Merely puppets, the rulers of Highgate are a façade for the city's true rulers, the Umbers.

## SYNOPSIS

Player characters enter Highgate and immediately notice that despite its external appearance, something is deeply wrong with the city. Plagued by an affliction being called "the gorgon's touch," which disorients people and turns them to stone, the city banishes those who have—or are suspected to have—the affliction. Some demand a cure, but most are just scared for their loved ones.

A ravenfolk woman named Spinel Larkdon, mother to a child with the gorgon's touch, begs PCs to save her child. An artifact known as the Shroud of Tiberesh, capable of curing any sickness, is locked away within the Umbers' vault of spoils below the city. Spinel is passionate and determined to save her son and all those afflicted.

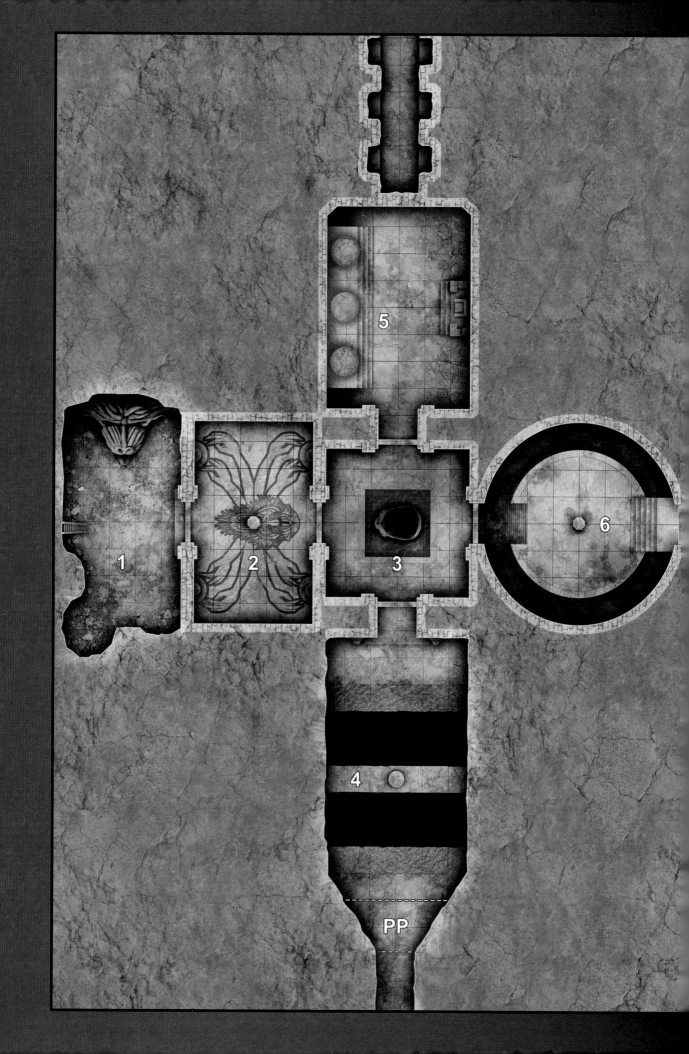

She explains that the shroud could heal and even completely reverse the effects of anyone affected by the gorgon's touch. A vocal group of citizens also believe the Umbers' treasure horde may hold something magical or powerful enough to rid the disease. However, none of the aristocrats or city officials will do anything to retrieve it. Officials say there is no guarantee that raiding the Umbers' lair would produce anything useful, and that drawing the ire of the cult would surely cost more lives than it would potentially save. Some of the braver residents of Highgate attempted to infiltrate the Umbers' gauntlet themselves, but wound up either found as corpses riddled with knife wounds, or simply never seen again.

Lord Vermin and his cronies aren't aware that one of the seemingly mundane baubles among the hundreds within their vault is so powerful. They have so many items they can barely keep track of them all. But it is their treasure nonetheless, and they don't like to part ways with their spoils. Fortunately for the PCs, surviving the Umbers' gauntlet means they are entitled not only to entrance into the cult but also to a single item from its vault of spoils, thanks to a longstanding part of their code. The PCs' best hope of procuring the shroud is by traversing this initiation gauntlet—a series of traps, monsters, and puzzles devoted to the demon-god Nakresh—and claiming the shroud as their prize.

PCs have several motivations for attempting to run the gauntlet and win the shroud, and they have more than one route of entry as well: they can infiltrate it either undetected or by posing as prospective cultists themselves. Should they survive the gauntlet, defeat its guardian, and obtain the shroud, they will be rewarded handsomely.

Even if the PCs succeed, they realize too late they've been pawns in a much larger scheme of Sister Starkfeather's. This, in turn, could spawn an entirely new adventure!

# PART 1: ROCK AND A HARD PLACE

The adventure opens as characters are traversing the Lotus Trail, headed either north toward Per-Bastet or south toward Per-Kush. Allow the group to come up with their own reasons for traveling together. Perhaps they are a nomadic group of entertainers or a specialized team of "tomb liberators." Maybe they formed a bond after surviving a perilous event together, such as exploring the Tomb of Tiberesh or meeting an angry djinn.

*In the distance ahead through the undulating heat, you see the tall walls of the city known as Highgate. Its white limestone walls glow under the midday sun.*

The PCs journey on the Lotus Trail has had its fair share of hardships Stopping at Highgate is advisable should they want enough water and supplies to survive their travels.

If the player characters insist on not stopping for some reason, tell them their characters will surely die of exposure to the elements as the nearest civilization is at least 2 days' journey from here. Should they still refuse, explain each of their deaths from heatstroke in lurid detail.

Once they've decided to head toward the city:

*As you approach the looming perimeter of Highgate, you notice there are many stone statues outside its walls. Depictions of men, women, and children in various poses grow in number the closer you get to the entrance. Some are in the fetal position, some are on their knees, and some are embracing one another.*

Characters investigating any of these statues do not need to attempt a check to notice they are immaculate depictions of the various races that inhabit this region. However, a PC who succeeds at a DC 17 Perception or DC 12 Craft (sculptures) check notices that some of the statues appear slightly moist in places, as if made from clay that is not fully dried.

If a player character gets a particularly high result (exceeding the DC by 10 or more), she hears one of the statues make a muffled sound.

## THE STONE SICKNESS

Also referred to as "the gorgon's touch", this disease is transferred through the sharing and/or contact of bodily fluids with someone who is already afflicted. So far, there is no known cure for the disease, although some in Highgate believe there is magic powerful enough within the thieves' guild vaults to help.

## ENTERING THE CITY

Upon entering the city, the characters should immediately notice, amid the typical hustle and bustle of the city, everything here is not exactly as gleaming and bright as it seems from the outside.

*Horse- and camel-drawn carts steadily trot along the stone streets before you. The smell of freshly baked bread wafts through the air as children run about and play, and vendors boast about their wares loudly from their stalls.*

*Louder however, is the voice of a dark-skinned dwarven man standing atop a barrel. He rings a bell and holds a sign that reads in bold lettering, "ANU AKMA COMES".*

Allow the PCs to briefly soak in their surroundings. Interacting with the dwarf man should clearly let the players know:

- His name is Badul, and he believes the city is succumbing to a divine plague.

- People are slowly turning to stone, starting with a small patch of dry skin that quickly spreads and turns their entire body to chalky white stone within a few days' time.

- City officials are doing almost nothing to help and are simply urging citizens to stay indoors until the sickness has run its course.

Whether they interact with Badul or not, after the PCs are in the city for a few moments, read the following.

*The bazaar at the city gates is peppered with various statues like the ones outside. Some lay in corners, others lie prostrate on the sandstone streets. People bustle past the statues without looking at them, many covering their mouths with handkerchiefs or makeshift masks.*

## MEETING SPINEL (HOOKS)

The PCs' next action should be interrupted by Spinel Larkdon, a ravenfolk woman with reddish grey plumage and a beak that has a deep gouge in its left side. If the players decide not to approach or interact with Badul, Spinel relays the same information.

*"Travelers!" A somewhat shrill and fragile voice erupts from the hum of the city. "Please, a mother begs of your aid. My son suffers with a terrible sickness. A mother cannot simply stand by and watch her only child slowly turn to stone! No one in this forsaken city of thieves will risk their own neck to help, but perhaps you will? I can make it worth your while."*

Spinel is dressed in sandy-colored hooded robes tied off with a simple white sash. Her eyes are a pale blue and filled with desperation. The player characters can question her as they see fit; keep the following in mind.

- Spinel is genuinely concerned about saving a young boy named Etiryp who has the stone sickness, although he is not actually her son. He is the son of a friend of hers, Galena, who came to her for help. Etyrip is in the middle stage of the disease's progression and has only about 24 hours before it consumes him.

- The Umbers have a hold over the city. They are a guild of thieves dedicated to a cult of the demon-god Nakresh and devoted to thievery and magic. Any character succeeding at a DC 10 Knowledge (history or local) check learns whatever portions of the History and Background section you'd like to reveal.

- She is familiar with the cult of Nakresh and its gauntlet because she is a member herself, serving Sister Starkfeather. She passes this knowledge off with a convincing story about how Lord Vermin's associates troubled her family for decades. (A DC 25 Sense Motive check reveals she's telling a partial truth. Her clan skirmishes with Vermin.)

- She claims a family heirloom artifact (the Shroud of Tiberesh) was stolen by The Umbers several years ago, and without its healing properties, her sister passed away. This story is absolutely false, but Spinel shares it with the conviction of one who's told a lie so many times that they themselves believe it. A PC who succeeds at a DC 25 Sense Motive check realizes this. Spinel refuses to acknowledge that her story is false.

- She has more than adequate monetary and magical resources to pay the characters handsomely for the artifact's return (within reason), and she considers it a paltry price to pay for aiding Sister Starkfeather while simultaneously avoiding risking her own life.

## THE JOB

If the characters show interest, Spinel asks them to speak more privately and invites them into her nearby home. If they are reluctant to enter her home, she offers a more public venue in a partially secluded corner of the market. In either case, she then discusses the job more in depth.

*"Thank you, thank you so much. Now, we're going to need to recover a magical artifact that once belonged to my family. Stolen by Lord Vermin's filthy little insects, it is a burial shroud of a once-powerful sorcerer king that has immeasurable restorative and preservative powers."*

Spinel explains that the Shroud of Tiberesh is hidden within the Umbers' maze, and that not only will it help save Etiryp, but it could also potentially reverse the effects of the sickness for those who are already stone.

Spinel says that those who survive the Gauntlet not only are granted entrance into the Umbers but can also take a single item from the guild's hoard at the end of the trial. This treasure serves both as a prize and as proof of survival. This is of course not the only way to retrieve the Shroud, as breaking in and finding a way to the hoard is also an option. She laments that she would do it herself if she were the bird she was 20 years ago.

She offers to pay 300 gp per character, as well as a small cache of minor magic items (GM's choice) equal to the number of PCs for them to divide among themselves as they choose. If the PCs agreed to meet in her home, she shows them the cache by motioning toward a locked chest and showing them a sample from within. Otherwise, she does not specify the items but assures the characters they are quite valuable.

Spinel is wealthy, although she doesn't really look the part, and she can be bargained with. A PC who succeeds at a DC 16 Diplomacy check convinces her to pay more, and she offers an additional 100 gp per character. A result of 21 or higher causes her to offer the Shroud of Tiberesh to the characters after Etiryp is cured, should they do a particularly efficient job of acquiring it. Failing the check by 5 or more causes her to become irritated, and she'll no longer increase the reward.

If pressed for provisions, Spinel offers the PCs two *potions of cure light wounds*, basic ammunition, rations, and torches.

For combat purposes, should unwise characters attempt to cross or harm Spinel, she is a 13th-level sorcerer. Additionally, her friend Galena is a crimson-feathered ravenfolk rogue 6/assassin 3 who arrives to assist her 1 round after combat begins.

Repeatedly prying or accusing Spinel of falsehood will only anger her; each time a player character does so, decrease the amount of gold she offers by 10% and remove a minor magical item from the treasure cache. Additionally, each time this happens, reassure the players that Spinel seems genuine.

# PART 2: GETTING DIRTY

Once the characters have agreed to help, whatever their motivations, Spinel provides them with a means to escape the gauntlet swiftly once they've obtained the shroud.

*"Take this scroll; it was a gift from my mother's grandfather long ago. It was he who planned to infiltrate the cult's gauntlet, steal their most prized possessions, and whisk himself away. The spell inscribed here will teleport your group to safety once you've got what you need."*

The script on this *scroll of word of recall* is written in a dead language and it functions solely to return its travelers to the permanent circle within Spinel's family home.

*"Now, as for gaining entrance to the Umber's gauntlet and claiming its prize. You can either sneak your way in or pose as initiates. The Umbers have little faith in outsiders who wish to prove themselves. They assume such hopefuls will perish almost instantly, so they let most anyone into the trial without much regard."*

Spinel advises the characters there are two main ways to gain entrance into the Nakresh Gauntlet—either through stealth or by posing as prospective cult initiates. If they wish to pose as cultists, they can approach the gauntlet directly through the entrance below the bazaar at the center of town; proceed to the Deceptive Route section that follows.

However, if they opt to take a stealthier approach, there are two little-known routes through the sewer that can provide concealment and entrance into the gauntlet. One is known as the "Deadman's Slough" and is accessed through a grate at the center of the Graveyard District. The other is accessible just outside the stables through a massive sinkhole and is referred to as "Geb's Maw". If the PCs prefer one of these approaches, proceed to the Stealthy Route section that follows.

## DECEPTIVE ROUTE

If the players decide to pose as cultists, read the following aloud as Spinel.

*"Have your wits about you. You'll need to give the impression of utmost devotion to the '8-armed Demon God Nakresh, his hands grasp all there is to take and hold.' Head straight to the Umbers' gauntlet foyer by speaking with Corvus, one of their fences who runs a shop as a cover. He's set up in the bazaar."*

After speaking with the characters about their approach, Spinel takes a few moments to provide them with a rough hand-drawn map indicating where to find Corvus, and the entrances she's described. Proceed to the Corvus's Tent section that follows.

## STEALTHY ROUTE

If the characters decide to sneak into the Umbers' gauntlet, Spinel says the following.

*"You've two options for sneaking in: through either the Deadman's Slough in the Graveyard District or Geb's Maw. The graveyard is a bit less conspicuous, but the area underneath is surely guarded by something unliving."*

Spinel tells characters inquiring about Deadman's Slough the following.

*"Beneath a grate near the back of the Graveyard District, by the old king's tomb, there is a tunnel that should lead you directly into one of the chambers within the Umbers' gauntlet."*

Spinel tells characters inquiring about Geb's Maw the following.

*"Between the stables and the slums, a massive sinkhole breaches the city streets. Not many go near it for fear it will widen and swallow them whole. At its bottom is a sewer tunnel that leads to the Umbers' gauntlet."*

Allow the characters to make any final requests, ask questions, and so on before they set out to enter the gauntlet. Proceed to the either the Deadman's Slough section or the Geb's Maw section, depending on the entrance chosen by the group.

## CORVUS'S TENT

Characters seeking out Corvus will easily find him as marked on Spinel's map. His shop is an octagonal black tent with gold trim, each side having an embroidered shape of a hand on it. Upon entering, read the following aloud to the characters:

*Standing inside and idly admiring his own jewelry is a finely dressed roachling man with a pompadour haircut of thick, wiry hair, and well-polished shoes. He regards you with a wide smile as his antennae stand up from his well-groomed hairdo. "What can I do for ya?"*

The PCs can interact with Corvus for a bit; use the following to guide those interactions.

- Corvus is a man of stature within Lord Vermin's ranks. He is a faithful and tenured guild fence. He is primarily concerned with the moving of goods and his own self-importance.
- He does not know of Spinel personally, as all of Sister Starkfeather's acolytes are all the same to him.
- He does not know of the Shroud or many specifics of the guild's gauntlet, beyond being glad he was grandfathered in before the trial became mandatory.
- He takes the intake of initiates into the gauntlet very seriously, and he only allows those who prove their true devotion to Nakresh to pass.
- He knows that typically, Umber initiates come one or two at a time; an entire party of initiates is uncommon, and often a red flag.
- When taking payments given as a show of devotion to Nakresh, Corvus doesn't care about the source, so long as they have some value. Every little bit helps Lord Vermin's cause.

If the characters approach Corvus as an entire group, they must prove themselves worthy. Doing so requires each of them to succeed at a DC 15 Diplomacy or DC 14 Bluff check before he will even consider them for admission. A PC can intimidate him by succeeding at a DC 24 Intimidate check instead.

If the characters approach Corvus individually, or after the group has proven themselves to him, they must show their "devotion" to Nakresh simply by donating an item of their own or by procuring one from a stranger in the bazaar. Once the PCs have done this and convince Corvus to let them through, read the following aloud.

Corvus pulls back the fine gnollskin rug on his floor, revealing a hatched sewer entrance. Well-kept and relatively free of grime, the foyer you descend into has four heavily armed guards, two roachling and two gnoll, who stand watch over the gauntlet's entrance. The hatch closes and seals above you.

### Development

If the party attacks Corvus, he flees, but he tells no one in order to save face. Otherwise he is still there if they return via his shop, congratulating them on their success.

Proceed to area A, Vermin's Vestibule in Part 3. (If the PCs pursued a fleeing Corvus, they face the guards in this area.)

## DEADMAN'S SLOUGH

Marked with a skeletal hand on Spinel's map, the Graveyard district holds the most discreet entrance to the Umbers' inner workings, but it is dangerous.

*The limestone streets here are cracked and choked with brambles and loose sand. At the base of a tall marble statue depicting an old king lies a simple brass grate and ladder. Hollow whispers of air float up from beneath.*

## KING'S ANTECHAMBER

This entrance leads into the old king's tomb and is guarded by unliving servants. The ladder descends into a 10-foot-by-10-foot featureless room that smells of rot and dust. A simple wooden door here gives way to a much larger 30-foot-square antechamber filled with monsters and a floor littered with crumbling limestone.

### Creatures

The antechamber contains a wraith, a ghast, and four zombies that attack on sight.

### Development

Beyond this room lies a narrow, linear series of hewn stone crypts that lead to a dead end. The dead end is actually a secret revolving door (requiring a D.C. 18 Perception check to locate) which leads into the Gauntlet's chapel.

Proceed to area C, Chapel of Chance, in Part 3.

## GEB'S MAW

Not long ago, a sinkhole opened up just within the city's walls near the stables. Many locals thought this was a sign from the gods. In reality, the subterranean foundation of the city was merely settling, and unfortunately a nearby homestead was swallowed up.

At the bottom of this massive sinkhole, which is roughly 20 feet in diameter and 150 feet deep, lies a shattered home, its debris strewn across the natural chasm.

Should characters decide to enter this way, they may draw a crowd of onlookers swept up in fear and awe. They will also require climbing tools, magic, or some other means of securing themselves as they travel downward. Climbing the unsettled earthen walls requires a successful DC 15 Climb check.

The bottom of the sinkhole is devoid of light. Once a light source is illuminated, or for characters with darkvision, read the following aloud.

*From the bottom of the sinkhole, a short dog-leg tunnel leads to a natural chasm about ten feet wide. On the other side, a torch-lit entrance to the sewer ducts gleams. This jagged tear in the earth descends to unknown depths. Across it lies splinters of a broken home and a ruined support pillar from the city walls above.*

The chasm is a straight drop for another 300 feet, and what lies at the bottom is certain death. Read the following if characters further inspect the boards and succeed at a DC 12 Perception check.

*The boards that stretch across are unfit to support the weight of even a dog without crumbling.*

A character can use the crumbled support pillar to form a makeshift bridge to cross the gap by succeeding at a DC 16 Strength check to move the pillar; each PC who crosses must succeed at a DC 13 Acrobatics check to traverse without falling. A PC who fails this check by 5 or more must succeed at a DC 15 Reflex saving throw or potentially fall to her death, taking 20d6 points of falling damage.

After half of the party has crossed the gap, they encounter 3 hungry gricks hiding amid the rubble (requiring a successful DC 16 Perception check to spot). Read the following aloud.

*The silence here is suddenly pierced by chittering and suckling sounds as three tentacled snake-like creatures slither outward. Their bodies' colors shift like chameleons as they detach from the rubble they hide in.*

### Creatures

The gricks are trained to remain in this area and do not pursue parties who escape.

### Development

After crossing the chasm, Proceed to area E, Demon's Gambit in Part 3.

# PART 3: THE GAUNTLET

Any who wish to serve the Umbers (and in turn, Nakresh) must complete this gauntlet in order to become a member. Located deep below the city, within segregated sections of decommissioned sewer, lies a series of linked chambers filled with traps, challenges, and monsters. No matter which path the PCs take, they must complete all five trials in order to unlock the vault of spoils and prove themselves worthy. Each chamber contains one of the five keys required to open the vault.

Each key should have a different description, so feel free to be creative with the shapes—a skeletal hand, a shooting star, or an acid-breathing dragon. However, the portion of each true key to be inserted is triangular in shape. Keep the descriptions filled with details, and only mention this if a player asks for specifics about that portion.

Unless otherwise noted, all doors are unlocked, not trapped, and lit by torchlight sconces. Additionally, resting is not an option during this event, as saving the boy is time sensitive. Should characters consider taking a rest, remind them it will cost Etiryp his life.

## 1. VERMIN'S VESTIBULE

Descending from Corvus's tent is a short trip; once characters reach the bottom read the following aloud.

*This massive cave holds a gigantic carving of a demonic baboon face, its tongue sticking outward. A half-dozen armed guards stand before you, seemingly ambivalent to your presence. Flanking an iron door with pull-rings, gnolls brandish polearms and roachlings each wear a bandolier of daggers. Shortswords rest at their hips, and they do not speak or make eye contact.*

Interacting with the guards here won't elicit much of a response. They tell the characters to move into the gauntlet or get out. The guards, like most, assume the characters will not survive long.

## Creatures

Ensure the PCs are aware of the relative power of the four gnolls (each a 6th-level barbarian) and two roachlings (both are rogue 6/assassin 2); this should deter the PCs from attacking.

## Development

Once the characters have entered, read the following aloud and proceed to area B.

*The iron doors creak shut with a low rumble of metal against stone. From the other side you can hear the muffled sound of a board being slid across the threshold, barring you inside.*

### 2. NAKRESH'S GRASP

Meant as an initial test to those who enter the Umbers' gauntlet, this is a very apparent testament to those who follow Nakresh's ways. Five bronze keys lie within plain sight, but four of them are false, and they are all guarded by very real traps.

This relief on the floor here is one representing Nakresh and his eight arms, grasping all that he can hold. The pillar in the center holds one of the five keys in this room, although it is false. It is also trapped (see Pedestal Trap on page 26). The true key sits on the shelf in the southeast pillar (4) that Nakresh's lower left hands are grasping.

*This chamber of smooth stone is home to a carved relief of a massive beast upon its floor. At its center, a simian face with its mouth agape holds an octagonal pedestal that rises about 3 feet. Two bodies lie propped up against it. Directly across the chamber is another door.*

Characters who inspect the bodies and succeed at a DC 10 Heal check learn the halflings have both been dead for approximately 1 week. One appears to have been killed by a crossbow bolt to the head. The cause of death of the other, who is much older, cannot be determined. A successful DC 11 Perception check uncovers a hand crossbow, 4 bolts, a small pouch filled with sand, two daggers, two suits of leather armor, and two plain iron wedding bands.

If the characters ask for more details about the room, read the following aloud.

*You notice the relief includes eight arms that snake along the floor in pairs of two, each set branching toward four separate columns that run floor-to-ceiling at the northwest, northeast, southwest, and southeast corners of the room.*

These 4 columns at the northwest, northeast, southwest, and southeast are attached to the walls, flanking both doors. Marked on the map as 1 through 4, each is painted with a different scene, and each contains a small shelf holding an identical triangular bronze key. Column 4 holds the real key.

The columns each depict an aspect of Nakresh's aspects.

**1. Brazen Theft**: Hooded figures stealing from paupers and elderly.

**2. Magical Treasure**: Piles of glittering gold, wands, weapons, and baubles.

**3. Power**: An insect holding a blade in its pincers and sitting atop a throne.

**4. The Exalted**: One hooded figure, stealing from another dressed identically.

Columns 1–3 are trapped and can't be disarmed:

1. Removing this key instantly ages the first person who touches it 3d6 years (DC 20 Will save negates, but the victim's hair turns white on a successful save). It is infused with necromantic magic that can be spotted with *detect magic* or with a successful DC 15 Knowledge (arcana) or DC 25 Perception check.

2. A burst of sour-smelling golden miasma bursts from a crack in the wall here. Creatures adjacent to the pillar must succeed at a DC 20 Fortitude save or become fatigued and sickened for 1d6 hours. For each hour that passes while the victim suffers from this effect, it must succeed at an additional DC 20 Fortitude save or become exhausted. Noticing this trap requires a successful DC 25 Perception check.

3. A mechanized spear bursts out of the column from a recess behind a hollowed surface, jabbing at whoever stands directly in front of the pillar (Atk +15, 3d8 piercing damage; DC 25 Reflex halves). Spotting this trap requires a DC 20 Perception check.

4. Characters hear a deep metallic click followed by a faint rumble from somewhere deep within the walls. Nothing happens.

## Pedestal Trap

Removing the key from the central pillar causes a weight-sensitive plate to trigger the crushing ceiling trap, which causes the 20-foot-high ceiling to slowly descend.

| CRUSHING CEILING TRAP | CR 7 |
|---|---|

**Type** magic; **Perception** DC 31; **Disable Device** DC 31

**EFFECTS**

**Trigger** touch; **Reset** manual

**Bypass** Placing the key or something of similar weight (4 pounds) causes the ceiling to ascend 5 feet on initiative count 20, until it reaches the ceiling's height of 20 feet.

**Effect** The ceiling descends at a rate of 5 feet per round after triggering on initiative count 20. When the ceiling has descended 15 feet, all Medium or larger creatures must succeed at a DC 21 Reflex save or fall prone. When it descends 20 feet, it deals 20d6 points of bludgeoning damage to all creatures in the room.

### 3. MAGICMONGER'S MENAGERIE

The central chamber to the Umbers' gauntlet is dedicated to the strange arcane puzzles wizards of Nakresh adore.

A massive obsidian skull sits in the center of the room, and faux gemstones made of glass are set into the stone floor below it. By adorning the skull's third eye with the proper gemstone, the PCs can release the key that is held in a protective stasis above the skull. Using the wrong gemstone may result in certain death—or mighty amusement.

Regardless of entry point into this chamber, read the following aloud.

*This perfectly square chamber has a high ceiling and doors on each wall. At its center, sitting in a shallow pool cut into the floor, is a huge obsidian skull. Floating high above it within a small magical force field is a triangular bronze key.*

The skull itself was carved from a single chunk of obsidian. Its mouth frozen in a grin, it has two massive cannonball-like gemstones, ruby on the left and sapphire on the right, for eyes. Each gemstone weighs 85 pounds and can be removed by succeeding at a DC 25 Strength check. At the center of its forehead is a third eye, carved depicting eyelashes and a centered gaze. Characters succeeding at a DC 12 Perception check notice there is a shallow divot in the center eye where the pupil would be.

The key is suspended 10 feet above the skull, and the skull itself is roughly 4 feet tall. Characters attempting to climb, fly, or otherwise reach the key cannot interact with it as the magical barrier surrounding it acts as a *wall of force*. The only way to dispel the barrier is to pluck the proper gemstone from the floor and put it into the inset of the skull's third eye.

Read the following aloud when characters make a closer inspection of the area surrounding the skull.

*The skull sits in a shallow, water-filled pool cut a few inches into the floor here. Beneath calm ripples you notice a series of colorful fist-sized gemstones, which are also set into the floor.*

The gems are arranged in a straight line from left to right under the shallow water: quartz (clear), red, orange, yellow, green, blue, purple, black. Each of these "gemstones" are simply cut and dyed glass made to resemble similarly colored gems such as ruby, citrine, onyx, and have no value. This can be deduced via a successful DC 15 Appraise check, but only after one of the gems has been removed from its inlay and properly inspected. The gems can easily be pried from their settings with a dagger, knife, or anything thin enough to wedge between them and their inlays in the floor.

The combined colors of the skull's eyes provide the solution to the puzzle, so purple is the correct gemstone to remove and place in the skull's third eye. Upon doing so, the force field above flickers out, and the key crashes to the ground with a metallic clang.

When other gemstones are placed within the eye, different effects take place (see below). These cannot trigger more than once, and removing a gemstone will not reverse its effects once triggered.

- **Quartz.** The PC who placed the gemstone has his lungs immediately filled with water and begins suffocating.

- **Red.** A portal opens from the back of the skull and an incubus demon crawls forth, attempting to drag a PC back into the hells with it. It fights to the death.

- **Orange.** A *fireball* (CL 9th, 9d6 points of fire damage, DC 14 Reflex halves) explodes from the skull's nostrils.

- **Yellow.** Lightning leaps out in all directions, filling the room and effecting every creature inside per the effects of *chain lightning* (DC 19 Reflex save halves) starting with the character who placed the gemstone. Creatures standing in the shallow pool around the skull take an additional 2d6 damage.
- **Green.** *Stinking cloud* (DC 14 Fortitude negates) erupts from the skull's mouth.
- **Blue.** The entire room is temporarily plunged through the arcane veil as a decapus skitters into existence as *black tentacles* (CL 7th) erupt around the skull for 5 rounds. Fighting to the death, the decapus uses its sound mimicry ability to taunt the party.
- **Black.** Unnatural darkness dims the torchlight in the room. A single neh-thalggu flickers into view, seeking to devour the character with the highest Intellect. It fights to the death.

None of the creatures leave this room.

## WHEN THE FIRST WRONG GEM IS CHOSEN

Luckily, the characters won't be without at least a little help here. A *magic mouth* has been cast on this chamber's north wall. It can be easily spotted (DC 10 Perception check) by anyone looking at the north wall near the door. It triggers after the first time an incorrect gem is inserted into the skull's third eye. Read the following when this happens.

*Rock and dust crumble to the ground as an animated mouth on the north wall opens with a yawn. It speaks to you. "Travelers, perhaps I may be of some assistance?"*

The *magic mouth* does not operate as per the standard rules for the spell, in that this mouth has several preprogrammed responses. It promises to answer two questions that warrant a "Yes" or "No" response, provided they know one of the answers will be the truth, while the other will be an outright lie.

After being asked two questions, the wall recedes and doesn't reappear until the next set of hopefuls traverses the gauntlet.

## Development

As the core of the test, the party can pass through this area several times as they complete the other tests. As long as they do not reset the gems, they do not trigger further effects. Proceed to the appropriate areas.

### 4. DEMON'S GAMBIT

This chamber is also the byproduct of the Umbers being resourceful with the natural areas of their subterranean Gauntlet. This chamber holds its key atop a specialized bolt thrower that rains death onto those who enter the room, trapping its occupants inside.

Any PC entering this room notice that the ground near the chasm is covered in a translucent brown liquid with a successful DC 11 Perception check. This is nonmagical grease that makes traversing the chasm even harder.

## ENTERING FROM GEB'S MAW

If the PCs enter from the east, read the following.

*After traversing the sewers for some time, you find your passage widens and gives way to a room carved from a natural cave.*

*At the center of this chamber is a precipice of rubble-strewn rock that runs its entire width. Across it, you see a wooden door flanked by carvings of demonic simian faces. At the center of the precipice sits a cylindrical post with a bronze key atop it, glinting in the chamber's torchlight.*

Once characters step far enough into the room, a pressure plate (marked by PP in the dotted area on the map and requiring a successful DC 20 Perception check to spot) sends a portcullis from a recess above slamming down into the rock, trapping the characters inside the room. It is immensely heavy and requires a DC 25 Strength check to pull up. Once this happens, the **flechette volley challenge** activates.

## ENTERING FROM MAGICMONGER'S MENAGERIE

If the PCs enter from the west, read the following aloud after all characters have crossed into the room.

*The door behind you emits a deep click that reverberates through the chamber, locking you inside. The door is flanked by carvings of demonic simian faces, and directly across from you is a wide chasm interrupted by a thin precipice of rock. Across from that the room continues off into a perilous tunnel of darkness.*

After the characters have taken a few moments (from 1 to 3 rounds) to take in their surroundings and potentially notice the grease on the floor or take a closer look at the demonic faces on the walls, the flechette volley challenge activates.

The chasm (indicated by the heavily shaded dark areas) is over 200 feet deep and filled with jagged rubble at the bottom. Any creature falling into this chasm is likely killed by the 20d6 points of falling damage.

The ground in the areas adjacent to the chasms (indicated by dotted lines, lightly shaded) are regularly greased by Umber cultists; this terrain functions as though under the effects of a permanent *grease* spell.

The precipice at the center of the chasm is littered with rubble from bolt impacts and the natural degradation of the cave. It is considered rough terrain.

Each demonic simian face carving adjacent to the door (A, B) is a relief, depicted with its mouth agape. Each relief's tongue serves as a button; if both are depressed simultaneously, the flechette volley challenge stops for 1 round before resuming. The buttons are rather obvious and require only a successful DC 12 Perception check to notice.

## FLECHETTE VOLLEY CHALLENGE

Once the flechette volley challenge is activated, read the following aloud.

*A metallic \*SHING\* echoes sharply as mechanical grinding sounds fill the chamber. The cylinder at the center of the precipice whirs to life and begins launching thick iron quarrels in all directions, their impact biting tiny chunks out of the walls with each volley.*

The bolt thrower is a specialized mechanism, loaded with special flechette munitions. Every other round (1, 3, 5, and so on) on initiative count 20, it fires four heavy crossbow bolts (Atk +18, 1d10 points of piercing damage) in orthogonal directions. Each bolt is tipped with a glass bauble filled with acid that does an additional 1d4 points of acid damage in a 5-foot radius from its point of impact. Each other round (2, 4, 6, and so on), the bolt thrower rotates 45 degrees counterclockwise and reloads. It has enough ammunition to fire 30 times.

The shots fired from this mechanism can strike any creature within a 10-foot-wide path in the direction it is fired, striking the first creature or object in its path.

The bronze key sits freely atop the flechette volley mechanism, bouncing a tiny bit with each activation, but not enough to cause it to fall off. The door on the west wall remains locked (DC 30 Disable Device check) until the key is obtained and inserted into the lock.

### 5. CHAPEL OF CHANCE

Access to this chamber is possible through area D and through Deadman's Slough in Part 2.

This small crypt wasn't part of the Gauntlet when it was first built, but the Umbers have turned it into a shrine to their demon god. It also serves as an initiate's first test of loyalty. Cultists come here to pay tribute and beg favors of Nakresh, and in return they offer tribute in the form of coin, magical treasure, or nothing at all. Those who offer nothing place their lives in peril.

A skeletal servant of Nakresh guards this room, holding one of the keys needed to unlock the vault of spoils and also offering up a game of chance to those feeling particularly bold.

When the PCs enter, read the following aloud.

*Littered with rubble, this chamber is brightly lit by three large braziers on its south wall, with doors to the west and east. To the north sits a crumbled sarcophagus turned into a makeshift throne. Upon it sits a blindfolded skeleton; it turns and tilts its skull curiously at you as you enter.*

The skeleton sits motionless other than offering a roll of the dice it holds to each character, though only once each. The skeleton does not speak, and it vanishes in a burst of shimmering particles if threatened or attacked. After all characters have either rolled, passed, or made an offering, the skeleton sits back in its seat, dormant until it receives the next set of visitors.

When the characters approach the skeleton, read the following aloud.

*The skeleton holds its thumb and index finger in a circle, with its other 3 fingers fanned upward and places it over its blindfolded eye as if it were a monocle. Looking at you, it extends its other hand, which holds two blank, carved-bone dice.*

These *dead man's dice* it holds are useless if rolled separately. If taken from this room they vanish in a puff of iridescent smoke after crossing the room's threshold.

The braziers are meant for offerings; the brazier on the left has piles of coins, jewelry, and other valuables at its base. The one on the right holds a collection of small magical items such as enchanted daggers, wands, scrolls, and the like. The brazier in the center has only a shallow velvet-lined box at its base.

Characters who wish to make an offer to Nakresh can do so by leaving either any magic item or valuables worth at least 20 gp. Those who offer nothing must roll the dice offered by the skeleton into the velvet-lined box.

For those who roll the dice, consult the table below and feel free to vividly describe what happens to the character:

| 2d6 | Dead Man's Dice Effect |
|---|---|
| 2 | **Death**. Succeed on a DC 20 Fortitude save or take 15d6 negative energy damage. A creature that dies as a result is reduced to ash. |
| 3 | **Sickness**. Become nauseated for 15 minutes and then sickened for 1d6 hours. |
| 4 | **Hourglass**. Instantly age 10 years. |
| 5 | **Covetous**. Become overwhelmed with desire for others' belongings. |
| 6 | **Decay**. Take 1d4 Constitution drain. |
| 7 | **Luck**. Roll again twice, applying both effects. (This effect can only happen one per character). |
| 8 | **Visions**. Gain a +2 insight bonus on next attack roll, ability check, skill check, or saving throw. |
| 9 | **Quickness**. Roll twice on next Reflex save and take the best result. |
| 10 | **Brawn**. Gain a +1d4 enhancment bonus to damage with physical attacks until end of adventure. |
| 11 | **Wealth**. A random mundane item in the PC's bag turns to gold, worth 10 gp per pound of the item. |
| 12 | **Favor**. Roll twice on next three skill or ability checks and take the best result. |

## Development

The skeletal servant rewards the first character to make an offer of gold or magic item by giving her the key; she also gains a +1 luck bonus to all attack and damage rolls, ability checks, skill checks, and saving throws for the remainder of the adventure. Subsequent offerings allow characters

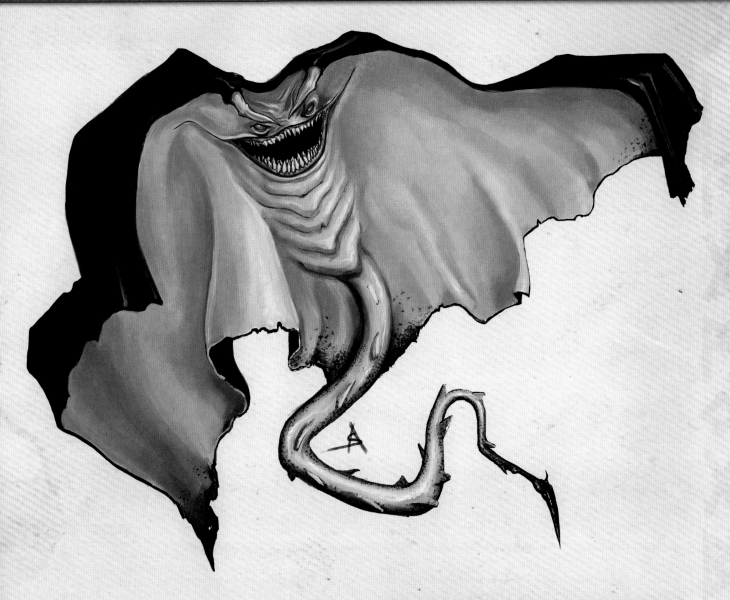

to roll twice and take the best result for an ability or skill check of their choice before the adventure's end. The character must choose to use this boon before making the check, and a character can receive this boon only once.

Those who attempt to steal from the offerings amuse Nakresh greatly, but the sheer audacity required to steal from the shrine of a god dedicated to thievery begets divine intervention. If this happens, the character who attempted to steal is unable to, and he is immediately affected by one of two random results of the dead man's dice, rolled on a single d6 (rerolling any results of 1).

Should the skeleton leave after being threatened or attacked, it still leaves a key behind. However, this key is cursed (requiring a successful DC 22 Spellcraft check to uncover), and you can secretly roll a d20 each time the character who carries it makes an attack roll or skill or ability check and take the lesser result until the party reaches area 6, the Hive.

## 6. THE HIVE

This final trial focuses around being able to kill or outwit whatever guardian lurks within it. The Hive is a circular chamber, dank, and filled with refuse and rubble. It is lined with mottled windows, outside of which hang the corpses of those who have come before and failed. The chamber serves both as a grim message to those who make it that far and as a means of storage for feeding whatever beasts currently reside as The Hive's guardian.

The guardian can be chosen randomly from the following table or determined ahead of time by the DM.

| d8 | Hive Guardian |
|-----|------------------|
| 1-2 | 1 Cloaker |
| 3-4 | 2 Basilisks |
| 5-6 | 2 Otyughs (Twins) |
| 7-8 | 2 Advanced Gricks |

29

## ROOM FEATURES

The perimeter of the hive is a ledge that rises 10 feet above the floor of the rest of the chamber. Sharp stairs on the north and south ends lead upward to this ledge. The floor below is strewn with rubble, sewage, offal, or whatever other bits the DM finds appropriate for the guardian, and is considered difficult terrain.

At the center of the Hive is a pedestal containing the final key required to open the doors to the vault of spoils. At the north end of the chamber atop the staircase is a massive brass door with five triangular keyholes; each must be filled with working keys in order to access 7. The Vault of Spoils.

The characters may manage a way to retrieve the key from the pedestal and open the door without fighting the guardian, or do so while it is distracted, restrained, or simply attacking them, but the door opens very slowly. It takes 4 rounds to open enough for Small creatures to fit through (or Medium creatures to squeeze through) and an additional 2 rounds to allow Medium creatures to easily fit through.

The room is fairly straightforward, depending on the particular enemy the party faces. You may want to adjust the following descriptive text accordingly.

*You enter into a huge circular chamber. Mottled glass windows line its circumference, and you can see down into an arena of filth. Outside the windows you see a small sea of corpses in various states of decay and hung on hooks.*

After the PCs look around the room for a moment, read the following aloud.

*A mechanized hatch from high above opens, and a few corpses fall through, their bones shattering on the surfaces below. A roar/bellow/rumble/growl vibrates the air…*

### Treasure

The creatures have no treasure, since it is in area G.

### Development

There is no other visible exit from this area. If the PCs make it through the locked door, proceed to area 7, the Vault of Spoils.

## 7. THE VAULT OF SPOILS

The vault is straightforward; should the characters reach this room, describe it as follows.

*Before you is an impressive chamber, filled with coins, jewelry, baubles, clothing embroidered with golden thread, magical weapons, wands, scrolls, statuettes, and just about anything else you can think of.*

Afterward, provide them the opportunity to search for the Shroud of Tiberesh, giving them a minute or two and describing the grandiose or odd things they sift through, before reading the following aloud.

*A thick shroud of burlap cloth lies here amidst scrolls and other papers. Faint stains mar its surface; they could vaguely resemble a face.*

A successful DC 19 Spellcraft or Knowledge (history) check reveals to the characters this is the item they're looking for. If proof is needed, any injured characters can hold the shroud near one of their wounds and feel it numb their pain. The characters can use their *scroll of word of recall* to return to Spinel.

Characters can also transport the corpses of any fallen friends when using the scroll. If dealings went particularly well with Spinel earlier in the adventure, she attempts to use the shroud to restore them to life.

After the characters have used the *scroll of word of recall*, proceed to Part 4.

# PART 4: STARKFEATHER'S DECEPTION

After using the *scroll of word of recall*, the characters find themselves instantly transported to the basement of Spinel's dwelling. She and Etiryp's mother are hovering over the boy.

*Spinel's feathers are ruffled and she is molting from stress. She rushes to you, "Do you have it? Oh, a mother begs you!"*

The characters should now turn over the Shroud of Tiberesh to Spinel. If they attempt to make further bargains with her, or refuse to give her the item she becomes extremely angry with them and demands the shroud. Reduce their reward by half.

Once Spinel has the shroud read the following aloud.

*Spinel takes the shroud and places it over Etiryp's face. Slowly, you see the petrified portions of his body recede and turn to flesh once again.*

*Tears run down Galena's face. She turns to Spinel and says "Thank you, thank you so much for saving him. My baby, he's going to live!"*

*Spinel gives a warm hug to Galena before seeing her up the stairs and out of the basement. She turns to you, a glint in her eye. "You have served Sister Starkfeather well, and Lord Nakresh will be very pleased"*

Let this settle in with the characters for a moment, and if they inquire further, have Spinel inform them of her background. She was genuinely concerned, although the boy wasn't hers, and this will further help Sister Starkfeather secure her victory against Lord Vermin in the upcoming trials. She asks the characters if they'd care to assist her further, or join with her and the Starkfeathers. Together they could rule this city and many more.

Spinel provides the gold and items as promised during their initial negotiation, and she even tosses in a little extra gold as a consolation if they are feeling too betrayed.

*"Awww, here you go… Keep your chins up; you could have done worse. You could have accidentally helped that filthy little derro, Zheita."*

This concludes the adventure. Proceed to Where to Go from Here?

## IF THEY FAIL

In the event that the characters did not return the shroud because they failed the trials or felt they could not survive, Spinel and Galena are greatly disappointed. They search the characters' belongings and then demand they leave. They then go on to gather other Starkfeather devotees to get the job done themselves. Unfortunately, the delay costs Etiryp his life.

## IF THEY HOLD BACK

In the event that the characters did not bring back the shroud in a bold-faced deception, Spinel and Galena attack, fighting to the death but likely overwhelming the PCs.

### Development

Should the party flee, Spinel tracks them and teleports after them later, to recover the shroud with prejudice. It should be an unpleasant encounter. If they give her the shroud and just flee, she hunts them later, helping their enemies for a year.

## WHERE TO GO FROM HERE?

There are now some pretty great threads for you to take and run with in your own Southlands campaign. Does the party:

- Attempt to stop Spinel?
- Join up with the Umbers and try and take them down from the inside? Or actually join the Umbers?
- Side with Starkfeather?
- Seek to re-obtain the Shroud of Tiberesh for themselves?

It's all up to you. Enjoy!

# BLOOD VAULTS OF SISTER ALKAVA

An adventure for four to six characters of 5th to 6th level
*by Bill Slavicsek*

## GM INTRODUCTION

Blood Vaults of Sister Alkava is an adventure that starts with the PCs performing an investigation for village elders and ends with a daring—and bloody—rescue attempt.

## BACKGROUND

Sister Alkava, one of the priestesses of the Red Goddess, has been utilizing necromancy and blood magic in an effort to impress her superiors in the priesthood and to garner the attention of the Elders of the Principality. To these ends, she created the Blood Vaults. She developed not only a method for prolonging the storage of fresh blood but also a way to draw power from the sacred Blood Cauldrons she uses in the storage process. That power motivated Sister Alkava to postpone the unveiling of the Blood Vaults and keep the news of her success to herself. She tasted the power, tested it, and drew it into herself. And she found the power intoxicating.

This year, as part of the Festival of the Verdant Tower, Sister Alkava collected the requisite tribute of blood from the people of the village of Karvolia. Unlike in previous years, however, none of the blood donors returned from the donation site. Moreover, the village elders have just been informed that a second tribute is required, and they have been commanded by the priestess of the Red Goddess to send another dozen young men and women to the edifice of stone that looms on the cliffs overlooking the village—the dreaded Blood Vaults of Sister Alkava.

The village elders are afraid of the Red Goddess and the vampiric Shroud-eaters, but they also don't wish to lose even more of their young people to the Blood Vaults, so they quietly put out the word that they're willing to pay adventurers handsomely to find a way to make this second tribute unnecessary. Unfortunately, by the time the brave adventurers respond, the latest set of donors has already entered the Blood Vaults and is being prepared for the donation process.

## ADVENTURE SUMMARY

The player characters must infiltrate the Blood Vaults, rescue the intended donors, and confront Sister Alkava—finding a way to stop her before her power grows too great to contain.

The adventure begins with a meeting with the village elders and the acceptance of a quest to save the young men and women who were recently marched into the Blood Vaults. Once inside the glorified mausoleum, the player characters explore the Blood Procession, the Bloodletting Chamber, the Donor Pens, the Storage Alcoves, and finally the Blood Cauldron Sepulcher, the massive chamber that Sister Alkava has turned into her seat of power.

## ADVENTURE HOOKS

Beyond the usual desire for reward, adventure, and experience, the player characters could have a variety of other reasons for deciding to aid the village of Karvolia. Here are a couple of examples.

**It's All Relative**. One or more of the PCs grew up in Karvolia and has a beloved relative among the donors sent to the Blood Vaults. For these PCs, the mission is extremely personal.

**A Matter of Church and State**. One or more of the PCs has been sent to investigate Sister Alkava by either the priesthood of the Red Goddess or the Elders of the Principality. In the case of the former, Sister Alkava's superiors grow increasingly concerned that they haven't heard from their priestess in months. They worry that Sister Alkava has gone rogue, and for good reason. The priesthood wants to know what Sister Alkava is up to, and they want her brought back to the Temple of Aprostala to answer for her infuriating silence.

In the case of the latter, the Elders of the Principality know that Sister Alkava was close to a breakthrough in necromantic techniques. When her regular reports stopped arriving, they feared she had stolen the research for her own purposes. This cannot be allowed to stand.

**Rebellion**. One or more of the PCs belongs to a secret group of freedom fighters working in the shadows to topple the governments of the undead. In particular, they seek to weaken or even end the rule of the vampires of the Principality. When they receive word of Sister Alkava's experiments to extend the Shroud-eaters' ability to preserve and store fresh blood, they know they have to destroy the process. And when they learn that the blood can also be used to increase the power of the vampires, they know that they must stop at nothing to put an end to Sister Alkava and her necromantic plans.

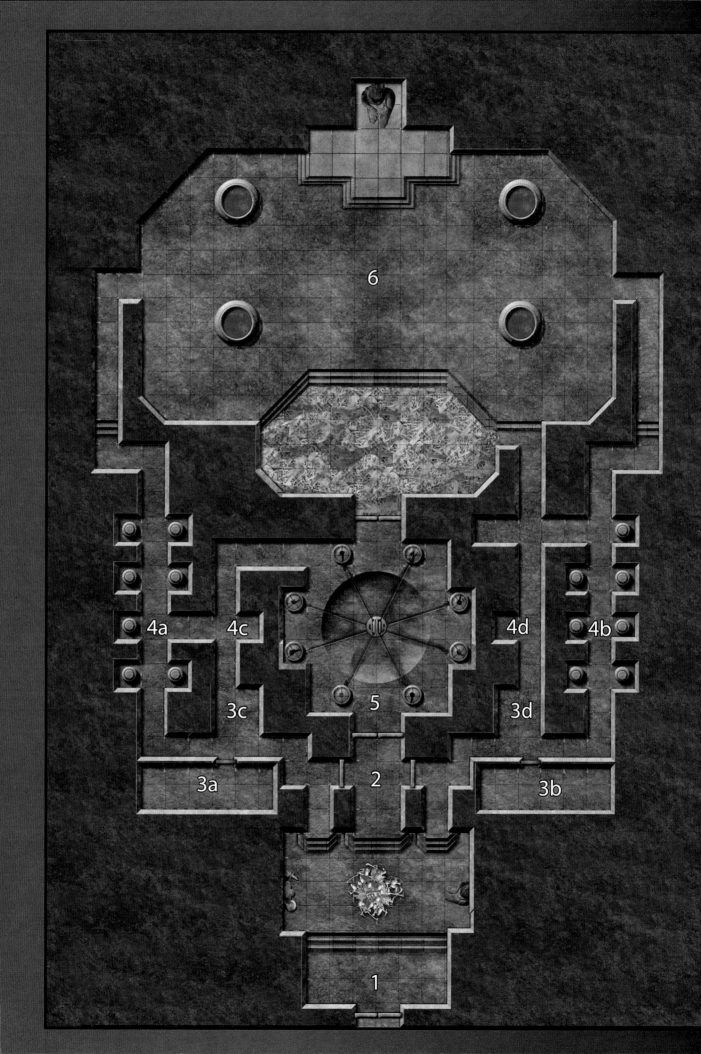

## THE VILLAGE ELDERS: A REQUEST FOR AID

The adventure begins as the player characters are spirited away to a back room of the Bleeding Crow Tavern to meet with Karvolia's council of elders.

*The back room of the Bleeding Crow Tavern smells of stale beer and old smoke. Lanterns hung at intervals along the walls provide muddy illumination, as there are no windows to let in either light or fresh air. Three ancient villagers study you from across a large wooden table—two men nursing tankards of ale and a woman who occasionally sips from a goblet of wine.*

The elders are the jovial Tanner Grimm, the nervous Olan Forn (who owns the tavern), and the stern Lady Bestin (who is neither noble nor courtly but earned her honorific by virtue of her age, her wealth, and the respect the villagers heap upon her).

The three take turns explaining the situation in Karvolia, relating what they know about Sister Alkava (which isn't much), the Blood Vaults, the secret work she's been performing these past few months, and the details of this year's Festival of the Verdant Tower.

*"Our initial tribute was accepted,"* Lady Bestin explains, *"but none of the donors returned from the Blood Vaults. When Sister Alkava demanded a second tribute, we knew drastic measures had become necessary. Save our young men and women, and a coffer of rare gems will be yours."*

The elders offer a small coffer of gems worth 2,000 gp—a fortune as far as the villagers are concerned—if the PCs can save the twelve young men and women who were marched off to the Blood Vaults less than twenty-four hours ago.

Before the PCs make the long trek out of the village and up the hill to the looming Blood Vaults, they might want to find out more information by talking to other people in the village. In general, the villagers appear nervous around the adventurers and obviously suspicious of their motives. They trust the village elders, though, and are willing to discuss certain matters, at least to some small degree. If the PCs approach the villagers politely and do their best to put them at ease, the PCs can learn the following information:

- Sister Alkava is a Red Sister, a priestess of Marena, the Red Goddess.
- The priestess came to the village a few months ago and immediately began her work to renovate the old Sanguine Shrine and turn it into the Blood Vaults.
- Blood Vaults have been popping up throughout the Principality as storehouses for the Shroud-eaters, but the villagers have reason to believe that Sister Alkava's Blood Vaults are special.

- The villagers suspect Sister Alkava is a necromancer due to the supplies she has commandeered from the village in the months she's been working in the old shrine.
- The village has faithfully provided blood tributes in the past, but this is the first time their loved ones didn't return after making their offerings.
- A second tribute was ordered by Sister Alkava. Another dozen young men and women have been escorted to the Blood Vaults—perhaps also never to return.
- Sister Alkava has at least a few living assistants, including a bugbear and a stony goblin.

## THE PATH TO THE BLOOD VAULTS

A well-traveled path leads from Karvolia up the hill to the cliffs overlooking the village. There, a looming edifice of stone that resembles a huge mausoleum seems to watch the village like a malevolent gargoyle. The final approach to the Blood Vaults, a cobblestone trail that cuts through the trees and winds directly to the massive stone doors, is protected by a hulking ogre zombie that Sister Alkava called forth specifically to guard the way.

The ogre zombie has been ordered to keep the villagers away while Sister Alkava finishes processing the most recent tribute. It bellows and blusters, deliberately swinging wildly to drive the PCs away if they try to approach the doors to the Blood Vaults. If the PCs attack the ogre zombie, however, it ignores its orders to do no harm and tries its best to injure or even kill the intruders.

| HILL GIANT ZOMBIE | CR 4 |
|---|---|

**XP 1,200**
NE Large undead
**Init** −2; **Senses** darkvision 60 ft.; Perception +0

**DEFENSE**

**AC** 19, touch 7, flat-footed 19 (−2 Dex, +12 natural, −1 size)
**hp** 54 (12d8)
**Fort** +4, **Ref** +2, **Will** +8
**DR** 5/slashing; **Immune** undead traits

**OFFENSE**

**Speed** 40 ft.
**Melee** slam +16 (1d8+12)
**Ranged** rock +6 (1d8+8)
**Space** 10 ft.; **Reach** 10 ft.

**STATISTICS**

**Str** 27, **Dex** 6, **Con** —, **Int** —, **Wis** 10, **Cha** 10
**Base Atk** +9; **CMB** +18; **CMD** 26
**SQ** staggered

# ENTERING THE BLOOD VAULTS

The cobblestone path leads up to a massive set of stone doors set into the walls of a massive stone structure. Gothic flourishes decorate the walls, but the bas relief of the Red Goddess carved into the doors strikes anyone who views it as both impressive and disturbing in its details.

The locked doors require a successful DC 20 Disable Device check to pick the complicated lock. Moreover, Sister Alkava placed a trap upon the lock.

| POISON NEEDLE TRAP | CR 6 |
|---|---|

**Type** mechanical; **Perception** DC 25; **Disable Device** DC 20

**EFFECTS**

**Trigger** touch; **Reset** none

**Effect** Atk +15 ranged (1d2 plus purple worm poison)

Once the PCs deal with the trap and the lock, they can enter the Blood Vaults.

## 1. ENTRY CHAMBER

A small vestibule leads up into the main portion of the Entry Chamber, a 20-foot-tall room with three arched openings that provide access into the facility.

*Tall statues on the right and left walls portray different aspects of the Red Goddess. The statue on the right depicts Marena as the goddess of sex and childbirth, showing an alluring temptress clearly pregnant beneath her filmy gown. The statue on the left represents the goddess as the patron of the realm, a wicked dagger in one hand and a decanter of blood in the other, firmly in control of death and suffering. On the far wall, two small archways stand to each side of a wider and taller archway, revealing corridors that lead deeper into the Blood Vaults. Piles of bones lie scattered between the two aspects of Marena.*

If any of the PCs inspect the arches more closely, read the following.

*The central arch stands fifteen feet high and ten feet wide. Carved droplets of blood decorate the arch, appearing almost as crimson drops of rain that frame the passageway. The arches to either side stand ten feet high and five feet wide, and are unadorned.*

Any PC who succeeds at a DC 15 Knowledge (history) check recognizes the central passage as the Blood Procession of the Red Goddess, the traditional path taken by supplicants and other donors intent on making an offering of blood to Marena and the Shroud-eaters.

When the PCs begin to climb the stairs into the main portion of the Entry Chamber, the bone piles animate and form into six distinct skeletons, each prepared to defend the Blood Vaults from intruders.

**Treasure**: One skeleton wears a tattered pouch on a threadbare belt that holds a transparent piece of pale blue quartz. A second skeleton has a small, round chunk of blackest obsidian stuck into its right eye socket. These gemstones are worth 10 gp each.

## 2. THE BLOOD PROCESSION

The central, 10-foot-wide corridor beneath the 15-foot-high arch leads to a set of double doors made of stone. Smaller stone doors separate the wide corridor from the eastern and western passages.

*Carvings on the double doors show the Red Goddess at the head of a blood procession, arms outstretched, welcoming supplicants and donors ripe with rich, warm blood. Lifelike paintings of even more donors, packed tightly together and marching toward the doors, decorate every inch of the walls, floor, and arched ceiling using perspectives that make everything seem to flow to the north.*

*Without a sound, an undead form emerges from the wall and slides toward you.*

This long hallway serves as the facility's Blood Procession, the path freely traveled by donors willing to give their blood to support the Elders of the Principality.

A spectre haunts the Blood Procession, a remnant of a donor who died in the process of providing sustenance to the Shroud-eaters in years past when this was still a Sanguine Shrine. The spectre, composed of undying hatred fueled by its untimely death, strikes at any living creatures in the hallway that aren't under the protection of Sister Alkava—in this case, the PCs.

## 3. DONOR PENS

The eastern and western passages leading away from the Entry Chamber and the Blood Procession provide access to the Donor Pens where Sister Alkava keeps supplicants prior to sending them into the Bloodletting Chamber (area 5 on the map).

**Area 3A: Male Donor Pen**. A dark, dank chamber accessed through an iron gate in the western passage contains two male supplicants who have not yet been sent to the Bloodletting Chamber. Olak Forn, son of the tavern owner and village elder, and Bruf Gaeron, an apprentice at the blacksmith's forge, cower in the cell as the domovoi guard (a stony goblin) watches from the shadows of area 3C. The domovoi enjoys taunting and terrorizing the supplicants.

If the domovoi hears the sounds of battle (against the skeletons, specters, or both), it prepares for the intruders by using its invisibility spell-like ability so that it can strike with surprise if the PCs approach its location. It won't leave its post unless ordered to by either Sister Alkava or the bugbear guarding area 3D.

**Area 3B: Female Donor Pen**. A dark, dank chamber accessed through an iron gate in the eastern passage contains the two female supplicants waiting their turn to enter the Bloodletting Chamber. Ara Kellt, daughter of the village brewer, and Jolla Rann, who operates a small tailor shop, stand defiantly in the cell, badgering the bugbear (in area 3D) and demanding to be released immediately.

The young women's constant demands
make the bugbear increasingly angry, almost
to the point where it's ready to swing open the
gate and throttle the two supplicants. If it becomes
aware of the PCs, it calls for the domovoi and rushes
to attack. (The bugbear is slightly smarter than the
tougher domovoi and has become the de facto leader of
the pair.)

**Secret Doors**: Secret doors set in the north walls of areas
3C and 3D open onto hidden passages that lead deeper
into the Blood Vaults. The domovoi and the bugbear don't
know about these secret doors, which date back to when
the place was a Sanguine Shrine. A PC can spot a secret
door with a successful DC 20 Perception check while
searching the chambers where the bugbear and domovoi
spend the bulk of their time.

**Treasure**: The domovoi confiscated pouches that belong
to the two male prisoners. They contain gemstones and
coins totaling 120 gp. The bugbear keeps a potion of cure
moderate wounds hidden in an old boot resting in the east
corner of area 3D.

| DOMOVOI | CR 6 |
| --- | --- |

**XP 2,400**

CN Medium Fey

**Init** +5; **Senses** low-light vision; Perception +11

### DEFENSE

**AC** 20, touch 12, flat-footed 18 (+1 Dex, +1 dodge, +8 natural)

**hp** 68 (8d6+40)

**Fort** +6, **Ref** +7, **Will** +8

### OFFENSE

**Speed** 30 ft.

**Melee** 2 slams +12 (2d6+4)

**Space** 5 ft.; **Reach** 10 ft.

**Spell-Like Abilities** (CL 8th; concentration +11)

  At will—*alter self, invisibility*

  3/day—*deeper darkness, dimension door, haste*

### STATISTICS

**Str** 19, **Dex** 13, **Con** 18, **Int** 6, **Wis** 10, **Cha** 16

**Base Atk** +8; **CMB** +11; **CMD** 25

**Feats** Dodge, Improved Initiative, Iron Will, Toughness

**Skills** Bluff +14, Intimidate +14, Perception +11, Stealth +12

**Languages** Dwarven, English, Trade Tongue

## 4. STORAGE ALCOVES

Alcoves in the eastern and western passages contain
huge stone urns that stand about 4 feet high and almost
5 feet wide. These urns hold much of the precious blood
that Sister Alkava collected during this season's festival.
Strange arcane symbols decorate each urn and its heavy
stone lid. A successful DC 20 Knowledge (arcana)
check lets a PC determine that the markings aid the
magic that somehow keeps the blood fresh and
pure. Exceeding the check DC by 5 or more
also allows a PC to determine that the
magic links each of the urns to some
other vessel of power elsewhere
within the Blood Vaults. When the
PCs enter one of these areas, read the following.

*Alcoves line the passage ahead. All but one of these recessed
spaces contains a large stone urn, its top covered by a heavy stone
lid. Strange symbols decorate each urn, unreadable runes that
seem to vibrate if you look at them too long. A faint metallic
tinge hangs in the air.*

**Area 4A: Western Alcoves**. Every alcove except for the
one containing the secret door holds one of the massive
urns. A successful DC 20 Strength check is required to lift
one of the heavy stone lids so the PCs can peer inside an
urn. Thick, rich blood, magically fresh and as viscous as
when it spilled from a supplicant's veins, fills each urn.

If the PCs examine the empty alcove, they can find the
secret door with a successful DC 20 Perception check.

One of the storage urns (marked with an "x") contains a
blood pudding, a creation of Sister Alkava's necromancy
that has been growing within the enchanted blood. It
dislodges the heavy lid and flows out to attack while the
PCs search the empty alcove or when they pass by the
blood pudding's urn.

**Area 4B: Eastern Alcoves**. The urns are the same as the
ones described in area 4A, and the secret door can be
found as described above.

The storage urn marked with an "x" in this hall contains
a blood pudding. It dislodges the lid of its urn and flows
out to attack when the PCs search the empty alcove or
when they head toward the northern passage.

This hall has one additional guardian. A blood zombie
stalks the corridor, patrolling from the top of the northern
passage to the beginning of the eastern alcoves and back

again. Anyone who succeeds at a DC 10 Perception check notices the elaborate blood-covered scabbard attached to a belt around the zombie's waist. (See Treasure below.)

If the blood zombie spots intruders, it immediately attacks.

**Areas 4C and 4D: Hidden Passages.** The secret doors can each be found with a successful DC 20 Perception check.

## BLOOD PUDDING

A blood pudding resembles a heavy mound of sticky, crimson sludge. In dim passageways, it appears to be little more than a pool of tainted water or a slick of spilled blood. Like a vampire, a blood pudding craves hot, fresh blood. It draws the blood out of its victims, leaving nothing behind but a dry and withered husk.

| BLOOD PUDDING | CR 5 |
|---|---|

**XP 1,600**
N Large ooze
**Init** −2; **Senses** blindsight 60 ft.; Perception -1

**DEFENSE**

**AC** 7, touch 7, flat-footed 7 (−2 Dex, −1 size)
**hp** 66 (7d8+35)
**Fort** +7, **Ref** +0, **Will** +1
**Defensive Abilities** amorphous; **DR** 10/bludgeoning or piercing; **Immune** acid, fire, negative energy, ooze traits

**OFFENSE**

**Speed** 30 ft., climb 20 ft.
**Melee** slam +8 (2d6+6 plus blood drain and grab)
**Space** 10 ft.; **Reach** 10 ft.
**Special Attacks** overflow
**Spell-Like Abilities** (CL 7th; concentration +3)
  Constant—*spider climb*

**STATISTICS**

**Str** 19, **Dex** 7, **Con** 19, **Int** —, **Wis** 8, **Cha** 2
**Base Atk** +5; **CMB** +10 (+14 grapple); **CMD** 18 (can't be tripped)
**Skills** Climb +12

**SPECIAL ABILITIES**

**Blood Drain (Ex)** On a successful slam attack, a blood pudding deals 1 point of Constitution damage. If a blood pudding begins its turn grappling a creature, it instead deals 1d3 points of Constitution damage. The blood pudding gains 5 temporary hit points for each point of Constitution damage dealt (up to a maximum number of temporary hit points equal to its full normal hit points); these hit points last for 1 hour.

**Overflow (Ex)** If a creature adjacent to a blood pudding hits it with a melee weapon, part of the pudding flows over the creature, dealing 1d3 points of Constitution damage (DC 19 Fortitude negates) and granting it temporary hit points as per its blood drain ability. If a blood pudding takes damage from a magic weapon, it cannot use this ability until the end of its next turn. The save DC is Constitution-based.

## BLOOD ZOMBIE

A blood zombie has been infused with necromantic magic that gives it a semblance of life. A thin coating of flowing blood covers the zombie as a shower of crimson constantly pours down its head and body.

| BLOOD ZOMBIE | CR 3 |
|---|---|

**XP 800**
NE Medium undead
**Init** −2; **Senses** darkvision 60 ft.; Perception +5

**DEFENSE**

**AC** 16, touch 8, flat-footed 16 (−2 Dex, +8 natural)
**hp** 25 (3d8+12)
**Fort** +5, **Ref** +1, **Will** +2
**Defensive Abilities** channel resistance +4; **Immune** undead traits

**OFFENSE**

**Speed** 30 ft.
**Melee** slam +5 (1d8+4 plus blood drain)
**Special Attacks** overflow

## STATISTICS

**Str** 16, **Dex** 7, **Con** —, **Int** 3, **Wis** 9, **Cha** 18

**Base Atk** +2; **CMB** +5; **CMD** 13

**Feats** Lightning Reflexes, Weapon Focus (slam)

**Skills** Perception +5

## SPECIAL ABILITIES

**Blood Drain (Ex)** On a successful slam attack, a blood zombie deals 1 point of Constitution damage. If a blood pudding begins its turn grappling a creature, it instead deals 1d2 points of Constitution damage. The blood pudding gains 5 temporary hit points for each point of Constitution damage dealt (up to a maximum number of temporary hit points equal to its full normal hit points); these hit points last for 1 hour.

**Overflow (Ex)** If a creature adjacent to a blood zombie hits it with a melee weapon, blood from the zombie flows over the creature, dealing 1d2 points of Constitution damage (DC 15 Fortitude negates) and granting it temporary hit points as per its blood drain ability. If a blood zombie takes damage from positive energy or a magic weapon, it cannot use this ability until the end of its next turn. The save DC is Charisma-based.

**Treasure**: If the PCs examine the urn in the western alcoves that released the blood pudding, they find an opaque yellow pearl worth 100 gp resting at the bottom of the blood-filled urn. The urns in the eastern alcoves contain only blood.

The blood zombie wears a +1 *short sword* in a scabbard at its side. Though the blade was a favored weapon in life, the zombie appears to have forgotten all about it and never uses it to attack.

## 5. BLOODLETTING CHAMBER

Doors depicting the Red Goddess at the head of an elaborate blood procession open to reveal the large, domed Bloodletting Chamber. Here, Sister Alkava and her servants collect blood for use in her necromantic experiments, instead of for the Elders of the Principality as was originally intended. When the PCs push open the doors or enter via the secret passage from the west, read the following.

*The domed chamber features a concave floor with channels carved into the stone that lead to a central drain. Eight tall metal cylinders, about the height and circumference of a large man, hang on chains suspended from the domed ceiling. Space remains between the bottom of each cylinder and the highest point of the curved floor, where the carved channels begin. Blood drips from holes in each cylinder's base, pooling beneath it before flowing down the rivulets and into the central drain. A clockwork automaton moves from one cylinder to the next, prodding it with a long wooden pole so that it swings upon its chain.*

In order to extract every drop of blood from the donors, Sister Alkava constructed these exsanguination cylinders. The eight cylinders each contain one of the young men and women who came to the Blood Vaults as part of the second call for a tribute of blood donors. The clockwork fellforged prods and swings the cylinders to ensure every drop of blood falls into the collection channels in the floor. With a successful DC 15 Perception check, a PC can hear muffled whimpers of fear and pain emanating from a swinging cylinder.

When the PCs arrive, three of the donors have already succumbed to the bloodletting and have died, but if the PCs hurry they can still save the remaining five.

To rescue a donor, a PC must move next to a cylinder and use a standard action to open the hinged door and set the victim free. By the time the PCs reach them, rescued donors are unconscious (and at –7 hp) from the loss of blood. Once freed, a donor must be stabilized or healed within three rounds (or succeed on a Constitution check [+0 modifier] to become stable) or he or she succumbs to the wounds caused by the exsanguination cylinder.

Any donors still inside the cylinders three rounds after the PCs entered the chamber must make a Constitution check (+0 modifier) to become stable at the start of every subsequent round. On a third failed check, a trapped donor dies.

When a metal cylinder is opened, a PC can see that the interior features hundreds of short, razor-sharp spikes designed to pierce the surface of the flesh and allow blood to freely flow. Holes in the floor of the cylinder give the blood a way to escape and drip into the collection rivulets carved into the floor of the chamber.

Necromantic spells cast upon the drain sends the collected blood directly to the Blood Cauldrons in area 6. If characters spend a moment to watch the blood flow into the drain, they see the blood swirl, fill the drain, and simply disappear.

**Defenders**: A fellforged, a clockwork construct given sentience by a captured wraith, tends to the exsanguination cylinders for Sister Alkava. It ignores the PCs until they either attack the fellforged or try to free one of the donors from a cylinder. When either of these conditions is met, the fellforged attacks.

## FELLFORGED

This brass automaton looks like a common gearforged, but its facial features carry a disturbing angularity that gives it an infernal cast. A darkly foreboding intelligence glows behind its eyes, and the entire being gives off an unsettling aura.

| FELLFORGED | CR 5 |
|---|---|

**XP 1,600**

LE Medium construct (evil)

**Init** +5; **Senses** darkvision 60 ft., low-light vision; Perception +10

## DEFENSE

**AC** 17, touch 11, flat-footed 16 (+1 Dex, +6 natural)

**hp** 53 (6d10+20)

**Fort** +2, **Ref** +3, **Will** +4

**Defensive Abilities** channel resistance +4; **DR** 5/good;
  **Immune** construct traits

**Weaknesses** exorcism sensitivity, light sensitivity

## OFFENSE

**Speed** 30 ft.

**Melee** slam +8 (1d6+3 plus 1d4 Con damage)

**Special Attacks** violent escapement

## STATISTICS

**Str** 14, **Dex** 12, **Con** —, **Int** 11, **Wis** 14, **Cha** 15

**Base Atk** +6; **CMB** +8; **CMD** 19

**Feats** Alertness, Combat Reflexes, Improved Initiative

**Skills** Perception +10, Sense Motive +7, Survival +5 (+9
  when following tracks); **Racial Modifiers** +4 Survival when
  following tracks

**Languages** Common

**SQ** unnatural aura

## ECOLOGY

**Environment** any

**Organization** solitary

**Treasure** none

## SPECIAL ABILITIES

**Exorcism Sensitivity (Ex)** While the body the fellforged
inhabits was constructed to specially bind spirits, the foul
presence of the wraith within is not invulnerable from
particularly strong clerics. The fellforged is considered a 5
HD undead creature versus any channeled turn attempts,
and the clockwork body shields the captured spirit
somewhat, granting it +4 channel resistance. Any successful
turn attempt exorcises the wraith from its clockwork frame,
but the creature is not bound by any further turn results,
even destruction, from this initial attempt. As the clockwork
body collapses lifelessly to the ground, the creature is now
treated as a wraith of the normal type in all respects and
may be subject to further turn attempts. The wraith retains
its current hp total.

**Unnatural Aura (Su)** All animals, whether wild or
domesticated, can sense the unnatural presence of fellforged
at a distance of 30 ft. They do not willingly approach nearer
than that and panic if forced to do so, and they remain
panicked as long as they are within that range.

**Violent Escapement (Ex)** With little regard for the clockwork
bodies they inhabit, fellforged wraiths can stress and strain
their mechanisms in such a violent manner that flywheels
unwind, gears shatter, and springs snap. As a move action
1/round, this violent burst of gears and pulleys can deal
2d6 damage to all adjacent foes (Reflex DC 15 for half;
Cha-based). Each use of this ability imposes a cumulative
–1 penalty on attack and damage rolls, skill checks, and
saving throws, and reduces movement by 5 ft. If its speed
is reduced to 0 ft. in this manner, the fellforged becomes
immobile and helpless until repaired. Repairing a fellforged
requires a DC 16 Craft (gearsmithing) check and the
expenditure of replacement parts worth 100 gp.

At the beginning of the next round after combat begins,
a vampire spawn loyal to Sister Alkava rushes into the
chamber through the northern doors to help defend the

exsanguination cylinders. It doesn't care
what happens to the fellforged; it wants only
to protect the blood donors until every drop
of blood has been fed to the Blood Cauldrons in the next
chamber.

**Rescuing Blood Donors:** For every blood donor that the
PCs save, including those kept in the donor pens, the PCs
gain 100 XP. No experience is awarded for donors who
die, either from exsanguination or by some other means.

## 6. BLOOD CAULDRON SEPULCHER

The massive chamber in the northern section of the Blood
Vaults is the Blood Cauldron Sepulcher. When the PCs
approach the doors to the sepulcher, read:

*The carved stone doors show an image of Marena the Red
Goddess in all her power and glory, providing the blood that
sustains the undead and keeps the realm safe. She stands amid
huge stone cauldrons that overflow with precious blood.*

When the PCs open the stone doors, or when they
approach the sepulcher from the passages to the east and
west, read:

*The massive chamber is divided into three distinct areas. An
octagonal entryway fills the southern portion of the chamber. Bas
reliefs of skeletal forms jut from the walls and reach down from
the ceiling, while the floor itself appears to be made of a carpet of
bones. Stairs rise out of the bones to the central area.*

The central area contains four large stone blood cauldrons. Blood bubbles and undulates in the cauldrons as magical energy sparks along the rune-carved floor.

A cross-shaped dais in the center of the northern wall features a magnificent and terrifying statue of the Red Goddess. Kneeling before the statue, her head bowed in prayer, is a priestess in bloodstained robes—Sister Alkava.

The climactic battle in the sepulcher can be complex due to everything happening in this chamber. The action is divided between the three key threats here: skeletons, blood zombies, and Sister Alkava.

**Skeletons**: When the PCs step onto the bone-covered lower level of the sepulcher, Sister Alkava's first layer of defense springs into action. (The skeletons don't automatically activate if the PCs arrive at area 6 by way of the east or west passages.) Read:

*The bone covered floor shifts and rumbles. Suddenly bones rise up and fly together, assembling to form eight distinct skeletons. The skeletons turn empty eye sockets toward you and rush to attack.*

The skeletons attack the intruders as Sister Alkava continues to pray at the statue of the Red Goddess. If the PCs remain in the lower level, they can deal with the skeletons without any other interference. But if any of the PCs step into the central portion of the sepulcher, the next layer of defense is activated.

**Blood Zombies**: When any of the PCs enter the central region of the sepulcher, read:

*The churning blood in the nearest stone cauldron bubbles over and a head rises out of the crimson depths. Blood flows down its face and neck as its dead eyes open wide. The rest of the body emerges as blood continues to run down its arms and chest. Then the blood zombie opens its mouth and screams.*

The first round in which any of the PCs enter the sepulcher's center region, the blood zombie inside the nearest cauldron emerges. It screams a terrible, mournful wail, an indication that it realizes the fate that has befallen it. These blood zombies were created from the bodies of some of the villagers who arrived as part of the first tribute, used to power the Blood Cauldrons and prepared in case Sister Alkava needed undead defenders. This one shambles toward the nearest PC and attacks.

In subsequent rounds, Sister Alkava uses a standard action each round to call forth another blood zombie. She does this each round until all four blood zombies have come into play. She can also use a standard action to activate the skeletons (two at a time) if the PCs didn't step into the lower level.

**Sister Alkava**: The entire sepulcher has been designed to augment and enhance Sister Alkava's power. She continues to pray before the statue of the Red Goddess until one or more of the PCs enters the central portion of the sepulcher. Then she rises and turns to face them. She never addresses the PCs directly. Instead, she carries on a conversation with the Red Goddess, a one-sided monologue in which she comments on the actions of the PCs, describes her own role in the events, and otherwise prays for guidance and support. Here are some samples of what she might say:

*"Look how they storm about our holy sepulcher, Red Goddess."*

*"Red Goddess, grant me your blood and your power!"*

*"That one insults you, Holy Mother. Let me smite him for you."*

*"I think that one would be perfect as a meal for my blood pudding."*

*"Their blood isn't worthy to fill these cauldrons, Crimson Mother."*

The Blood Cauldrons have been necromantically enchanted to increase Sister Alkava's power. Each Blood Cauldron provides Sister Alkava with the following benefits: +1 natural armor bonus to AC, 25 temporary hit points, and 1 extra standard action each round. While all four cauldrons are active, Sister Alkava has a +4 natural armor bonus to AC, 100 temporary hit points, and 4 extra standard actions every round. (Damage always targets temporary hit points first, if they are available.)

When the Red Sister uses an extra standard action, crimson energy rises out of one of the cauldrons and flows into her. She then releases that energy as either an extra move or attack action.

**Destroying the Blood Cauldrons**: If the PCs realize that the priestess draws power from the Blood Cauldrons, they can deny her some of that power by destroying the enchanted vessels.

Each Blood Cauldron has AC 10, 20 hit points, and hardness 10. When a cauldron is destroyed, Sister Alkava loses one point of natural armor bonus to her AC, 25 temporary hit points, and 1 extra standard action. If all the cauldrons are destroyed, she loses all the associated bonuses and benefits.

## SISTER ALKAVA

Sister Alkava is a priestess of the Red Goddess and a necromancer of skill and power. She wears scale mail beneath her bloodstained robes and wields a +2 *unholy mace*. Once completely loyal to the Elders of the Principality, her experiments with preserving and empowering blood have made her hungry for even more power and glory. She hopes to achieve a level of power that will either make the Elders offer her a place of prestige in the Principality or force them to leave her alone. Regardless, there's no way she's going to let a group of foolish adventures interfere with her plans.

| SISTER ALKAVA | CR 7 |
|---|---|

**XP 3,200**
Female human cleric 7
LE Medium humanoid (human)
**Init** −1; **Senses** Perception +4

**DEFENSE**

**AC** 15, touch 9, flat-footed 15 (+6 armor, −1 Dex)

**hp** 56 (7d8+21)

**Fort** +8, **Ref** +1, **Will** +9

**OFFENSE**

**Speed** 20 ft.

**Melee** +2 unholy heavy mace +8 (1d8+3)

**Special Attacks** channel negative energy 7/day (DC 17, 6d6), destructive smite (+3, 7/day)

**Domain Spell-Like Abilities** (CL 7th; concentration +11)

7/day—bleeding touch (3 rounds)

**Cleric Spells Prepared** (CL 7th; concentration +11)

4th—divine power, inflict critical wounds[D] (DC 18), unholy blight (DC 18)

3rd—animate dead, bestow curse (DC 17), dispel magic, rage[D]

2nd—death knell[D] (DC 16), hold person (2, DC 16), ray of the eclipse[DM], silence (DC 16)

1st—bane (DC 15), command (DC 15), ray of sickening[UM] (DC 15), shield of faith, true strike[D], voidmote[DM] (DC 15)

0 (at will)—bleed (DC 14), detect magic, guidance, resistance

[D] **Domain spell; Domains** Death, Destruction

**STATISTICS**

**Str** 13, **Dex** 8, **Con** 12, **Int** 10, **Wis** 18, **Cha** 14

**Base Atk** +5; **CMB** +6; **CMD** 15

**Feats** Command Undead, Extra Channel, Great Fortitude, Improved Channel, Toughness

**Skills** Intimidate +9, Knowledge (religion) +10, Spellcraft +10

**Languages** Common, Elven

**Combat Gear** potion of cure serious wounds; **Other Gear** +1 scale mail, +2 unholy heavy mace, phylactery of negative channeling

## CONCLUSION

After defeating Sister Alkava and her minions, the PCs should return to the village and claim their reward. If the PCs bring back proof that Sister Alkava has been defeated and news regarding the fate of the village's young men and women, or if they return any of the rescued donors safely back to the village, the elders remain true to their word and hand over a coffer filled with gems totaling 2,000 gp. The more victims from the second tribute they were able to save, the more grateful the elders are toward the PCs. In addition, the PCs receive 100 bonus XP for each villager rescued from the Blood Vaults.

What happens next depends on the relationship the PCs have with either the Red Goddess or the Elders of the Principality. Do they destroy the Blood Vaults? Do they try to restore the site to gain favor with the priesthood? Or do they report Sister Alkava's activities to the Shroud-eaters in hopes of earning an additional reward from the ruling class of vampires?

# CARRION SHRINE OF QORGETH

An adventure for five 6th-level characters set in the Western Wastes

*by James J. Haeck*

## GM INTRODUCTION

Qorgeth's fanatical undead followers await a messenger from their dark master. They whisper blasphemous prayers at blood-drenched altars in total darkness, their profane chants calling Qorgeth's demonic emissary to the mortal world. The unspeakable evil now threatening Midgard's Western Wastes was awoken by the well-intentioned mistakes of a man named Petring, a loving father who was seduced by Qorgeth's lies. It falls to a party of PCs to undo his cataclysmic mistakes and protect Midgard from the coming of a demon prince.

## SUMMARY

This adventure can be used to conclude the series begun in the Pit of the Dust Goblins and continued in the Crypt of Green Shadows, or it can serve as a stand-alone adventure. This adventure is most cohesive if the PCs are familiar with the children Rennie and Linde from the Pit of the Dust Goblins adventure and have heard of Petring, their father.

Petring was once a butler who served the lord and lady of Feycircle, but he withdrew from service when he began experiencing apocalyptic dreams. Every night, he saw Anax Apogeion—one of the Great Old Ones menacing the Western Wastes—swallow up his little town. He prayed to every god he could think of, but only Qorgeth responded. The demon lord manipulated Petring into corrupting the corpses of Feycircle's ancient dead into undead servants. When Petring began to resist, he outlived his usefulness, and the undead Wormhearts subdued him before continuing their profane quest to summon the malakbel demon, a messenger said to spread the corrupting word of Qorgeth until such time as the lord of worms can be summoned himself.

## FACTIONS

The following groups and individuals play an important role in this adventure.

**Wormhearts**. Qorgeth's most devoted servants, the Wormhearts, long to hear what they call the Utterance of Certain Decay, a word of power sacred to the Writhing **Prince**. The malakbel demon they summon will deliver it unto them. The wormhearted suffragans animated by Petring's misguided rituals single-mindedly pursue the tasks at hand: summoning the demon and killing their enemies (in order of importance). If Qorgeth's minions claimed any of the artifacts in the Crypt of Green Shadows, wormhearted suffragans in Area 8 use them against the PCs.

**Prisoners**. A number of prisoners—living, dead, and undead—are being held as sacrifices for the Wormhearts' summoning ritual. As a demon lord, Qorgeth demands living sacrifices, but as Prince of Decay, he also hungers for dead flesh. The zombified corpses of the living satisfy his needs well. Those prisoners who have not yet been ceremonially prepared and slaughtered are too weak to escape on their own, but they can reward the PCs if they are saved and returned home (see Area 4).

**Petring and his Children**. Petring has a special role in the Wormhearts' ritual: bait. Qorgeth's minions have been commanded to lure his innocent children and their heroic protectors to the ritual as grand sacrifices. Petring (human commoner 2) is a captive and longs for freedom, but he is tormented by guilt for what he's done. If sufficiently motivated (see Area 1), he joins the PCs and helps thwart the Wormhearts' profane scheme. Rennie (human commoner 1) is a precocious six-year-old and is full of childish bravado, though that bluster crumbles to panic at the first sign of danger. Ten-year-old Linde (human commoner 1) is a well of quiet determination, and her courage can grant inspiration to one PC when they need it most.

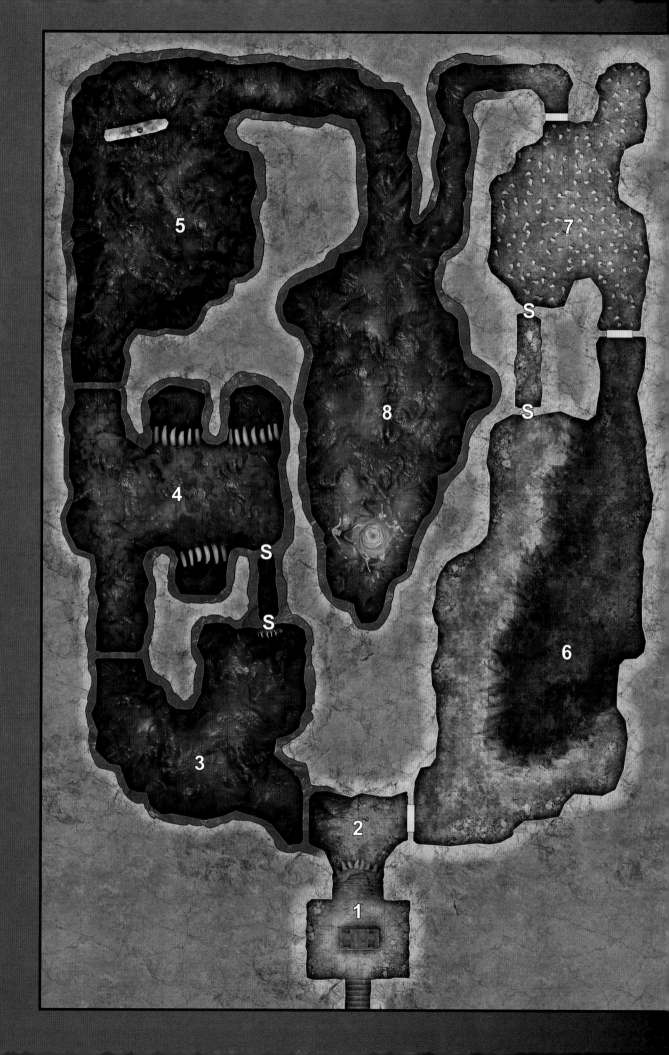

## ADVENTURE HOOKS

As GM, you know best how to involve the PCs in this adventure. The following adventure hooks are provided to inspire and assist you.

- **A Missing Father.** Following the adventure in the Crypt of Green Shadows, the PCs learn Rennie and Linde's father created a secret passage leading to a shrine beneath the crypt. Only the PCs' swift intervention can save him.
- **End of Act I.** A demon-summoning ritual is the perfect capstone for the lower levels of a long-term campaign. If the campaign isn't Qorgeth-focused, the Wormhearts may be the militant religious arm of an evil empire or the secret heart of corruption infesting a church of purity and light.

## ADVENTURE START

Unless otherwise noted, all areas in this dungeon are devoid of light. The descriptive text in this adventure assumes that the PCs have darkvision or a light source. The PCs descend two flights of crude earthen steps into a cramped passageway clearly designed for only one person's use. Immediately before them is a room lit by flickering torchlight.

### 1. INNOCENT ALTAR

*At the base of the stairs is a tiny chamber dug out from the surrounding earth. Looming in the center of the northern wall is a stone carving of a massive worm's toothy mouth. A dark tunnel leads through the mouth, and a stone altar stands in front of it. A motionless man is shackled to the slab. His fine silken clothes are spattered with blood and muck. Two torches flicker dimly on either side of the altar.*

The man shackled to the slab is Petring, and this shrine is of his own creation. The caverns just behind the gaping maw were dug out by the undead created through his rituals. He is unconscious, but stable at –1 hit point. If revived, Petring awakens in a state of panic, but a successful DC 25 Diplomacy check or the sight of his children calms him. Unshackling him requires a DC 20 Disable Device check or a DC 18 Strength check.

**The Children.** Rennie and Linde love their father dearly and are terrified by what has happened to him. They refuse to leave his side and beg recalcitrant PCs to forgive him. If the PCs wish to bring Petring into the dungeon with them, Rennie's eagerness may prove dangerous, though Linde's resolve can grant the effects of inspire courage (as per the bardic performance) for 6 rounds once per day.

## WHAT PETRING KNOWS

- He built this small shrine because he received apocalyptic dream-visions for weeks in which the Great Old Ones converged on Feycircle and destroyed everything and everyone. He gave in and created this shrine, as shown to him in the dreams. The tunnels through the worm's mouth aren't his creation.
- He is a prisoner of the undead priests that Qorgeth used him to create. They are conducting some damn awful magic in the tunnels. He doesn't know why he's kept out here.
- The Wormhearts keep talking about some "Uttering of Sudden Doom" and said they want a demon to tell it to them.
- Other prisoners are being kept in the tunnels somewhere. Some are alive, others are undead.

### 2. MOUTH OF QORGETH

*Inside the worm's mouth are two earthen tunnels; the eastern one is sealed by a stone door and the western is blocked by a wall of stinking flesh. Flies buzz throughout this chamber.*

Both tunnels lead to the Heart of Qorgeth, but only the western path is currently used by the Wormhearts. Petring has been dragged through the both tunnels countless times and knows prisoners are being held in the west, but he doesn't know why the undead priests refuse to enter the eastern passage anymore. He also knows the Wormhearts always say a certain phrase before opening doors in this place. He can't remember it very well: "Vosh tilloobum Qorgeth dar." A character who can speak Abyssal or who succeeds at a DC 14 Linguistics check understands he is trying to speak the Abyssal phrase "Qorgeth's messenger will come," correctly translated to "Va'ash tar'rupan Qorgeth ta." This phrase protects the speaker against the infestation trap on the walls of flesh along the western path.

**Eastern Door.** The eastern path was locked down when furious earth elementals rose from the soil and killed a Wormheart, setting its many undead thralls free. The iron door to this tunnel bears an ominous circle of Abyssal sigils, surrounding what looks like a handprint of dried blood. It is also locked, requiring a successful DC 20 Disable Device check to unlock.

**Inflict Wounds Trap.** The eastern door bears a deactivated trap. A PC succeeding on a DC 14 Knowledge (arcana) check learns a character can reactivate the trap either by casting *inflict serious wounds* on the door or by self-inflicting 13 points of damage and placing a bloody handprint within the ring.

## INFLICT WOUNDS TRAP                    CR 7

**Type** magic; **Perception** DC 31; **Disable Device** DC 31
### EFFECTS

**Trigger** proximity (alarm); **Reset** manual
**Effect** spell effect (maximized *inflict serious wounds*, DC 14
Will save for half damage)

**Western Door.** The western path is blocked by a wall of
rotting flesh. Tiny grotesque helminth worms audibly pop
as they writhe through its flesh. A door is carved into the
wall, with a handle of bone protruding from the flesh. The
door is unlocked and can be opened, but the opener may
be victim to its trap.

**Infestation Trap.** Parasitic helminth worms, like those
that live within the wormhearted suffragans' flesh, have
infested this wall of flesh. A creature that touches the
flesh or makes a melee attack against it without first
speaking a specific Abyssal phrase must attempt a DC
14 Constitution saving throw. On a failure, they are
infested by parasites. An afflicted creature can't regain

hit points and its hit point maximum decreases by 10
(3d6) for every 24 hours that elapse. If the affliction
reduces the target's hit point maximum to 0, the victim
dies. The affliction lasts until removed by any magic that
cures disease.

## HELMINTH INFESTATION TRAP              CR 7

**Type** mechanical; **Perception** DC 30; **Disable Device** DC 30
### EFFECTS

**Trigger** touch; **Reset** automatic (immediate)
**Bypass** speak Abyssal phrase "Va'ash tar'rupan Qorgeth ta"
**Effect** disease (helminth infestation)

## HELMINTH INFESTATION

**Type** disease, contact; **Save** Fort DC 15
**Onset** 1 day; **Frequency** 1 day
**Effect** 1d4 Con and victim cannot regain hit points through
rest; **Cure** 2 consecutive saves.

## 3. THROAT OF QORGETH

*This tunnel's "stone" smells like a decaying corpse and squelches when touched—it isn't made of stone at all. All around you is a cavern of rotten flesh. Four humanoid corpses partially protrude from the walls and ceiling.*

The undead embedded in the fleshy walls and ceiling of this tunnel silently survey all who enter. If a living creature not accompanied by a wormhearted suffragan enters this area, a group of four advanced plague zombies drop from the ceiling as a single wight pulls itself out of a squishy orifice on the floor.

**Walls of Flesh.** The northern door of this chamber is crawling with helminths and has a helminth infestation trap identical to the one in Area 2. Touching the walls, ceiling, and floor of this chamber is viscerally disgusting but not harmful.

**Secret.** The lifeless head of a giant worm protrudes through the northern wall, its jaw clenched tight like an iron vise. A successful DC 20 Strength check is required to force its jaws open. The decaying worm "tunnel" leads to the cells in Area 4, allowing sneaky creatures to ambush the undead guards there.

## 4. RIBS OF QORGETH

*Massive, yellow-white ribs grow from the floor and pierce the walls, creating three separate cages. All are filled with bodies; there is movement in one these cages, breathing coming from another, and only motionless bodies in the third. Three figures with ghastly white skin and wearing full armor stand guard between doors to the north and south.*

A trio of wights protect the Wormhearts' future sacrifices from living intruders. They were once mortal worshipers of Qorgeth trapped in undeath by some damning bargain, and they exist solely to drain souls from their living foes and transform them into undead abominations, just as Qorgeth did to them. They do not immediately notice intruders from the secret passage in Area 3, but prolonged noise, even whispering, draws their attention.

**Cages.** The northwest cage is filled with corpses. The northeast cage holds five placid zombies. The southernmost cage is filled with three living creatures. The first is a dust goblin raider named Wristsnapper that has no concept of subtlety or making a stealthy escape. One of her fellow prisoners is the last human captive from Feycircle, a grizzled hunter named Klegg who accepts rescue but tries to secretly kill Petring with a hidden knife for bringing this calamity upon his town. (A PC who succeeds at a DC 17 Sense Motive check discovers Klegg's intent, and a PC who succeeds at a DC 22 Diplomacy or Intimidate check can dissuade him from carrying out the murder.) The final prisoner is Nevamira, an elf adventurer from Dornig. She was staying in Feycircle to investigate the Crypt of Green Shadows when the blight hit.

**Walls of Flesh.** This chamber is made entirely of flesh and smells of vomit and acid, as if the stone itself was transmuted into a giant digestive organ. The walls drip with a corrosive ooze that deals 2d6 points of acid damage to anyone who touches it, and the helminth-infested door is identical to the helminth infestation trap in Area 2.

## 5. SHATTERED RIB OF QORGETH

*The fleshy walls of this room ooze metallic-smelling black ichor. A giant curved bone the color of spoiled milk has been turned into an altar in the north of the room. A shuffling sound made by multiple creatures comes from a tunnel to the northeast.*

When PCs examine the altar, read the following:

*This altar is caked with dry blood and covered with torn toenails, atop which rests a small clay bowl of squirming helminth larvae.*

If the PCs enter from the south, two wormhearted suffragans arrive from the northern passage, each dragging two corpses. They hiss when they see the characters, and one spends its first action to cast *animate dead* to turn the corpses into zombies while the other casts *hold person* on the best-armored PC. On subsequent rounds, one wades into combat while the other casts spells. The zombies attempt to take flanking positions to assist the suffragans.

If subdued, the Wormhearts mechanically repeat, "We await the messenger of the Devourer. We await the Utterance of Certain Decay."

| WORMHEARTED SUFFRAGAN | CR 4 |
|---|---|

**XP 1,200**

CE Medium undead

**Init** +7; **Senses** darkvision 60 ft.; Perception +11

### DEFENSE

**AC** 17, touch 13, flat-footed 14 (+3 Dex, +4 natural)

**hp** 37 (5d8+15)

**Fort** +4, **Ref** +4, **Will** +7

**Immune** undead traits

**Weaknesses** vulnerability to positive energy

### OFFENSE

**Speed** 30 ft.

**Melee** 2 slams +6 (2d6 plus disease)

**Special Attacks** disease

**Spell-Like Abilities** (CL 5th; concentration +8)

At will—*command* (DC 14), *detect good*

3/day—*inflict moderate wounds* (DC 15)

1/day—*animate dead*, *blindness/deafness* (DC 16), *hold person* (DC 15), *speak with dead* (DC 16)

### STATISTICS

**Str** 10, **Dex** 17, **Con** —, **Int** 11, **Wis** 16, **Cha** 17

**Base Atk** +3; **CMB** +3; **CMD** 16

**Feats** Combat Casting, Improved Initiative, Weapon Finesse

**Skills** Heal +8, Intimidate +11, Knowledge (religion) +8, Perception +11

### SPECIAL ABILITIES

**Disease (Ex)** *Helminth Infestation*: Slam—injury; *save* Fort DC 15; *onset* 1 day; *frequency* 1 day; *effect* 1d4 Con and victim cannot regain hit points through rest; *cure* 2 consecutive saves.

## 6. PIT OF CORRUPTED EARTH

*This wide stone chamber suddenly drops off into a pit of dark soil. Three large mounds of earth within churn with the speed and energy of swarming hornets.*

Unlike the rooms in the western passage, Areas 6 and 7 are made of stone and dirt, not rotting flesh and bone. The pit is 20 feet deep, with no obvious way in or out except a door to the north. Dozens of corpses were tossed into this pit for later use before this passage was sealed. The three mounds of dirt moving within the pit are Medium earth elementals driven mad by the corruption in these caverns. Bits of rotting human limbs protrude from them. When an elemental is killed, two zombies emerge from inside it and attack the nearest living creature.

**Trapped Door.** The northern door of this chamber is at the level of the pit and is made of thick stone. It bears a circle of Abyssal sigils and an uncharged *inflict wounds* trap (like the eastern door in Area 2).

**Secret.** A character who makes a DC 20 Perception check near the raised lip around the pit notices a dimly shining hunk of onyx protruding from the north wall. A character succeeding at a DC 15 Knowledge (arcana or religion) check realizes it is a receptacle for negative energy. When the gem takes at least 10 negative energy damage, it slides into the wall and creates a tunnel leading north into Area 7. The stone has 50 hit points.

## 7. GARDEN OF HANDS

*Dozens of skeletal hands protrude from this cavern's dirt floor, grasping the air as if for something just out of reach. Some clasp their bony fists tight around the motionless bodies of worms that are as long as a human's arm. A stone door stands to the north.*

Each 5-foot square in this room is filled with undead hands and is difficult terrain. Whenever a creature enters

BRYAN SYME

47

or examines a new space, roll 1d6 + 2 to determine the number of hands. The hands make a trip attempt whenever a creature enters their space, gaining a +1 bonus on their combat maneuver check for each hand in the space. If the hands successfully trip a creature, that creature takes 2 points of negative damage for each hand in its space at the beginning of its turn.

A space can be cleansed of hands by dealing 20 points of positive energy or fire damage. A space cleared of hands is no longer difficult terrain, but new hands sprout from the soil 1 round later.

**Trapped Door.** The northern door of this chamber is made of thick stone, and it bears a circle of Abyssal sigils and an uncharged inflict wounds trap (like the eastern door in Area 2).

## 8. HEART OF QORGETH

*The walls of the tunnel fade from dull grey and black to bright, bloody crimson. The walls pulsate, and the bass notes of a thunderous heartbeat rumble through the cavern, which resembles the atrium of a massive, beating heart. At the south end of the chamber swirls a vortex of color, fluctuating between sickly green, puce, gangrenous black, and yellow. Four wormhearted cultists of Qorgeth stand in small ventricles on the sides of the chamber, their heads lowered and chanting demonic verses. Each one is surrounded by a half-dozen corpses, already sacrificed. In the center of the atrium is an undead priest leading the incantation. Beside it is a coiled purple worm.*

The Wormhearts' ritual needs to continue for only 5 more rounds before the portal at the far end of the room stabilizes, allowing the malakbel demon to emerge. The ritual can be stopped only by killing or otherwise incapacitating all three wormhearted suffragans (the ritual leader and the cultists in the southernmost chambers). The young purple worm (use giant constrictor snake statistics) protects its master, but is not vital to the ritual.

If the ritual is halted, Qorgeth's power instantly begins to collapse. Any remaining undead disintegrate, and the fleshy, necrotic walls of Areas 3, 4, 5, and 8 wither away to nothing, causing these rooms to collapse after 1d6 rounds, dealing 10d6 bludgeoning damage to any creatures within them (DC 20 Reflex save for half damage).

If the ritual is completed, the malakbel demon tears through the portal in a burst of radiant black flame. The demon delivers a message to the cultists when it appears—the Utterance of Certain Decay.

*"The Writhing Prince, Lord of Decay, Devourer of All Things, will be reborn into the world of the living on the night when a consul of the Free City devours the heart of her rival. This knowledge has been spoken, and you have served your purpose, loyal servants. Embrace your reward."*

After delivering the Utterance, the malakbel demon attacks the undead servants of Qorgeth, granting them the decay they sought to bring to the world. Its Abyssal radiance makes short work of the Wormhearts, after which it turns its attention to the PCs. Depending on the size and strength of the party, they may be able to overcome it, at which point the Carrion Shrine of Qorgeth begins to crumble as if the ritual had been halted. If the PCs flee from the demon, it allows them to escape, preferring to see them sow fear and chaos by spreading rumors of Qorgeth's return.

---

### MALAKBEL DEMON                    CR 9

**XP 6,400**
CE Medium outsider (chaotic, demon, evil, extraplanar)
**Init** +3; **Senses** darkvision 60 ft.; Perception +19
**Aura** blistering radiance (30 ft., DC 20)

#### DEFENSE
**AC** 23, touch 13, flat-footed 20 (+3 Dex, +10 natural)
**hp** 114 (12d10+48)
**Fort** +12, **Ref** +11, **Will** +8
**Defensive Abilities** distortion; **DR** 10/cold iron or good; **Immune** electricity, poison; **Resist** acid 10, cold 10, fire 10; **SR** 20

#### OFFENSE
**Speed** 30 ft.
**Ranged** 2 ranged touches +15 (4d6 fire)
**Special Attacks** searing flare
**Spell-Like Abilities** (CL 12th; concentration +17)
  At will—*dimension door*

#### STATISTICS
**Str** 14, **Dex** 17, **Con** 19, **Int** 13, **Wis** 18, **Cha** 20
**Base Atk** +12; **CMB** +14; **CMD** 27
**Skills** Acrobatics +18, Appraise +16, Bluff +20, Intimidate +20, Knowledge (planes) +16, Perception +19, Sense Motive +19
**Languages** Abyssal

#### SPECIAL ABILITIES
**Blistering Radiance (Ex)** A creature that starts its turn within a malakbel's aura takes 2d6 points of fire damage (half of which cannot be reduced by resistance or immunity). The area within the aura is affected as per *daylight*.

**Distortion (Ex)** Ranged attacks have a 50% miss chance against a malakbel demon.

**Searing Flare (Ex)** Once every 1d4 rounds as a standard action, a malakbel demon can intensify its blistering radiance aura. All creatures within 30 feet of the demon take 6d6 points of fire damage and become fatigued (or exhausted if already fatigued as a result of this ability). A creature that succeeds at a DC 20 Fortitude takes half damage and does not suffer the fatigued (or exhausted) condition. The save DC is Constitution-based.

# CONCLUSION

The Carrion Shrine of Qorgeth can be the jumping-off point for a longer, Qorgeth-themed campaign. GMs looking to use it as a stand-alone adventure or the conclusion to a trilogy of short adventures can exclude this new plot hook. In this case, the Wormhearts intended to summon Qorgeth himself, but they overestimated their power and summoned a malakbel demon that sought only to destroy them.

Petring and his children can be reunited with their wife and mother in the refugee camp. If the PCs deem Petring worthy of punishment, it is their duty alone. The undead minions of decay had no use for wealth, but the villagers pool together their meager resources to offer the PCs a reward of 500 gold in mixed coinage and family heirlooms.

**Continuing the Adventure.** The worms and their masters are gone from Feycircle, the dead are at peace, and life is returning through the purified fairy ring. Rebuilding Feycircle may still require adventuring into the blighted Wastes. The prisoners from Qorgeth's shrine could all use assistance returning home, and they are fairly wealthy. Managing the personalities of sarcastic Wristsnapper and aristocratic Nevamira is an adventure of its own.

# THE LEYSTONE OF THE INDIGO STAR

An adventure for five 7th-level characters on the edge of the Western Wastes and the Magocracy of Bemmea *by Mike Shea*

## GM INTRODUCTION

The interrogation of the rogue wizard Askalan by the Magocracy of Bemmea exposed his creation of an unstable magical artifact built in a ruined ley line conduit. This Leystone, built by the mages of Vael Turog, had been dormant for centuries until Askalan discovered a way to power it. Now, after the wizard's untimely death, the Leystone's unstable power continues to grow at the edge of the Western Wastes. The Magocracy has hired the characters to find the awakened Leystone, uncover the mystery of this growing power, and return the source of the power to Bemmea for study.

It is highly recommended the adventurers include at least one character trained in Knowledge (arcana) and Use Magic Device.

## BACKGROUND

Askalan Graydust wasn't much of a wizard. Ignored by his superiors at the Magocracy of Bemmea, Askalan had been sent on missions of low importance and long travel for two decades. Upon one of his journeys to the edge of the Western Wastes, Askalan witnessed a miracle. A star fell from the sky, burning violet across the black night. At the crash site he found a being who looked like a newborn baby, though its semitranslucent skin revealed a network of glowing dark purple energy. Even the baby's eyes burned with violet light.

Slipping away from the Magocracy of Bemmea, Askalan raised the child and studied its strange origin. Three years after finding the fallen star Askalan found the key he needed to unlock the star's incredible power. Buried within the sands of the Western Wastes on the northwestern edge of the Field of Doors, Askalan found the remains of a ley line conduit built over a thousand years ago by the mages of Vael Turog. For two years Askalan worked to restore the Leystone, learning its secrets and rebuilding its arcane conduits. Two years later he placed the Indigo Star within its heart. The conduit flared to life, drawing energy from the ley lines that had long been dormant within the sands of the Western Wastes.

Askalan used the power of the Leystone to forge magical artifacts well beyond his skill. Returning regularly to Bemmea, he sold these items to unsuspecting wizards. Now these wizards have begun to die, their arcane energy devouring their bodies in a plague once thought eradicated centuries ago in the fall of Vael Turog. The Magocracy arrested Askalan and interrogated him. Though they learned of the existence of the empowered Leystone, Askalan died from the very arcane plague he brought back from the Leystone before he could reveal more information.

Now the Magocracy has hired a band of adventurers to locate the Leystone and bring the source of its power to Bemmea.

## ADVENTURE SUMMARY

The adventure begins when Finnius Kalarex, agent of the Magocracy of Bemmea, meets the characters in one of the glass gardens of Bemmea. Finnius wishes to hire the characters to locate the ruins discovered by Askalan. The Magocracy wishes to disable the Leystone before its power grows too great to control and to learn what they can from the source of that power.

In order for the PCs to locate the Leystone, Finnius gives them a ley line–sensitive chime and the use of a teleportation circle to take them closer to the edge of the Western Wastes. Before they use the teleportation circle, a band of fanatics from the Sons of Vael Turog attacks the characters in the hopes of stealing the chime and taking possession of the Leystone themselves.

Once they have defeated the fanatics, the characters travel into the Western Wastes and to the Leystone. Within the ruins, the characters must bypass the Leystone's protections and defeat creatures that still reside there. During their exploration, they learn of Askalan's research into the Indigo Star. Near the end of their journey, the characters must choose what to do with the Star before facing the Leystone's final threat, a void dragon named Ixaranum. With that foe defeated, the characters return to Bemmea and face the results of their choice.

## ADVENTURE HOOKS

Characters can get involved in this adventure in different ways. The following three hooks are examples of story threads that might draw the characters into the adventure. Tailor these hooks to suit the origins and drives of the characters or develop your own adventure hook based on their backgrounds and the history of the Leystone.

- **A Favor for the Magocracy**. Characters with ties to the Magocracy of Bemmea receive a summons from Finnius Kalarex. Finnius asks to meet the characters at the Twilight Gardens of the Academie Arcane in the city of Bemmea.
- **The Dark History of Vael Turog**. Characters discover the dark history of Vael Turog, the fallen city of mages, from before the Great Mage War and their experiments twisting the ley lines. Their research catches the eye of the Magocracy of Bemmea, who sends them a summons to aid in a mission of mutual interest.
- **Premonitions of a Growing Power**. One of the characters becomes overtaken with premonitions of a terrible growing power within the Western Wastes. She sees a black spire piercing out from the earth and hears the sounds of screaming echoing in her mind. She believes Finnius Kalarex of the Magocracy of Bemmea might have answers to her premonitions.

# PART 1: A REQUEST FROM THE BEMMEA MAGOCRACY

Whichever hook draws them to Bemmea, the characters arrive at the Twilight Gardens of Academie Arcana. When the PCs arrive, read or summarize the following:

*Beautiful trees sculpted out of violet glass and deep red crystal line the twisting path through the garden of the Academie Arcana. As the path turns, you see a huge statue of a serpentine monstrosity formed from shining red and black crystals.*

*"You like our andrenjinyi?" says a voice from behind you. You turn to see a middle-aged man with a receding hairline dressed in loose trousers and a silver-embroidered blue silk jacket that marks him as a ranking member of the Bemmea Magocracy. "You can't imagine the cost of imprisoning a beast like that." The serpent's crystal eyes blaze with red light. "Oh, she likes you! I am Finnius Kalarex, and I thank you for meeting with me."*

Finnius Kalarex takes the PCs to a gazebo within the gardens where servants serve fine wine along with aged cheese atop fresh bread. Finnius makes small talk as they eat, asking them how they like Bemmea and of their former adventures, before getting to the crux of his request. At that point, Finnius relays the following information to the PCs:

*Two weeks ago a low-ranking researcher of the Magocracy named Askalan Graydust returned to the city of Bemmea. He was a poor researcher often sent on long exploration missions alone. The Magocracy never expected much from him. Suddenly, this mage began to sell magical artifacts of power well beyond his capabilities. Some of those who purchased these items began to die, eaten by their own twisted arcane energy.*

After one such foul death, Askalan was arrested, subdued, and interrogated. His artifacts were investigated and, while the mages found no great danger from the artifacts, they feared these items could spell the beginning of a return of the arcane plagues of Vael Turog. During his interrogation, Askalan revealed the existence of the items' forge, located at a ruined Leystone at the edge of the Western Wastes. Before they could draw the exact location from him, Askalan's cursed body broke apart, consumed by the arcane plague he carried within him. The dangerous power of the Leystone, the mages discovered, continues to grow there after his death.

Finnius asks the characters to find the Leystone and disable the power growing within it. If they agree to help, Finnius gives the characters a small chime capable of guiding the characters to the Leystone. The chime is an item of delicacy and secrecy, he explains, and must be protected.

Finnius also provides the use of a teleportation circle located at a small observatory outside Bemmea that leads to a group of standing stones at the edge of the Western Wastes.

For their services, Finnius will reward the characters with one of three wands of the Magocracy (*lightning bolt, fireball*, or *dimensional anchor*) and a choice of three spell scrolls containing wizard spells up to 4th level, along with gemstones worth a total of 2,000 gp when they return.

## THE SONS OF VAEL TUROG

As they make their way out of Bemmea to the observatory containing the teleportation circle, the PCs are tracked by a spy of the Sons of Vael Turog named Sareth. It is possible a character spots the spy with a Perception check opposed by the spy's Stealth check. If the characters notice her and track her without being seen, they arrive at a fountain in a plaza. The Sons of Vael Turog have bribed the local guards to leave the plaza alone and plan an ambush there. Should the characters see the spy, they have a chance at scouting out the ambush before it happens. Two mages stand on nearby rooftops, one on each side of the plaza. Two additional spies lurk in the alleyways of the plaza.

If the PCs do not notice Sareth or lose her as they try to track her, they find themselves ambushed as they enter the plaza. The mages hurl *fireballs* and *magic missiles* at the characters while the spies try to attack spellcasters in the party.

The fountain itself is an arcane statue, depicting a former leader of the Bemmea magocracy, whose upraised hand sprouts colored water into the scintillating pool at the fountain's base. A large crack at the statue's base leaks arcane energy. A character within 5 feet of the statue can channel this energy as a move action by succeeding at a DC 19 Use Magic Device check. On a success, the character adds 3d6 points of force damage to any damage dealt by the next spell he casts this turn. On a failure, the character takes 2d6 point of force damage.

If the PCs successfully interrogate any of these assailants, they learn the attackers are from the Sons of Vael Turog and seek the ruined Leystone. Before the PCs get far into the interrogation, investigators of the Magocracy arrive and arrest the assailants with plans to perform their own interrogation; they suggest the characters continue on their way.

## SARETH — CR 6

**XP 2,400**
Female human rogue 7
NE Medium humanoid (human)
**Init** +8; **Senses** Perception +9

### DEFENSE

**AC** 19, touch 15, flat-footed 14 (+4 armor, +4 Dex, +1 dodge)
**hp** 56 (7d8+21)
**Fort** +4, **Ref** +9, **Will** +1
**Defensive Abilities** evasion, trap sense +2, uncanny dodge

### OFFENSE

**Speed** 30 ft.
**Melee** +1 shock short sword +7 (1d6+2/19–20 plus 1d6 electricity), mwk dagger +6 (1d4/19–20)
**Special Attacks** sneak attack +4d6

### STATISTICS

**Str** 12, **Dex** 18, **Con** 14, **Int** 13, **Wis** 8, **Cha** 10
**Base Atk** +5; **CMB** +6; **CMD** 21
**Feats** Dodge, Improved Initiative, Skill Focus (Stealth), Two-Weapon Fighting, Weapon Finesse, Weapon Focus (short sword)
**Skills** Acrobatics +14, Bluff +10, Disable Device +15, Disguise +10, Escape Artist +14, Intimidate +10, Knowledge (local) +11, Perception +9, Sleight of Hand +14, Stealth +17
**Languages** Aklo, Common
**SQ** rogue talents (distracting attack[APG], powerful sneak[APG], weapon training), trapfinding +3
**Combat Gear** potion of cure moderate wounds, potion of invisibility; **Other Gear** +1 studded leather, +1 shock short sword, masterwork dagger

## SPY (2) — CR 4

**XP 1,200**
Human rogue 5
NE Medium humanoid (human)
**Init** +8; **Senses** Perception +7

### DEFENSE

**AC** 18, touch 15, flat-footed 13 (+3 armor, +4 Dex, +1 dodge)
**hp** 41 (5d8+15)
**Fort** +3, **Ref** +8, **Will** +0
**Defensive Abilities** evasion, trap sense +1, uncanny dodge

### OFFENSE

**Speed** 30 ft.
**Melee** +1 short sword +7 (1d6+2/19–20), mwk dagger +6 (1d4/19–20)
**Special Attacks** sneak attack +3d6

### STATISTICS

**Str** 12, **Dex** 18, **Con** 14, **Int** 13, **Wis** 8, **Cha** 10
**Base Atk** +3; **CMB** +4; **CMD** 19
**Feats** Dodge, Improved Initiative, Two-weapon Fighting, Weapon Finesse, Weapon Focus (short sword)
**Skills** Acrobatics +12, Bluff +8, Disable Device +12, Disguise +8, Escape Artist +12, Intimidate +8, Knowledge (local) +9, Perception +7, Sleight of Hand +12, Stealth +12
**Languages** Aklo, Common
**SQ** rogue talents (powerful sneak[APG], weapon training), trapfinding +2
**Combat Gear** potion of cure moderate wounds, potion of invisibility; **Other Gear** masterwork studded leather, +1 short sword, masterwork dagger

## MAGE (2) — CR 4

**XP 1,200**
Human evoker 5
NE Medium humanoid (human)
**Init** +5; **Senses** Perception +6

### DEFENSE

**AC** 11, touch 11, flat-footed 10 (+1 Dex)
**hp** 40 (5d6+20)
**Fort** +3, **Ref** +2, **Will** +5

### OFFENSE

**Speed** 30 ft.
**Melee** mwk dagger +2 (1d4—1/19—20)
**Special Attacks** intense spells (+2 damage)
**Arcane School Spell-Like Abilities** (CL 5th; concentration +9)
7/day—force missile (1d4+2)
**Evoker Spells Prepared** (CL 5th; concentration +9)
3rd—fireball (3, DC 19)
2nd—elemental surge[DM] (2, DC 16), scorching ray (2)
1st—mage armor, magic missile (3), shield
0 (at will)—acid splash, light, mage hand, prestidigitation
**Opposition Schools** enchantment, illusion

### STATISTICS

**Str** 8, **Dex** 13, **Con** 14, **Int** 18, **Wis** 12, **Cha** 10
**Base Atk** +2; **CMB** +1; **CMD** 12
**Feats** Craft Wondrous Item, Elemental Focus[APG], Improved Initiative, Scribe Scroll, Spell Focus (evocation), Toughness
**Skills** Craft (alchemy) +12, Intimidate +5, Knowledge (arcana) +12, Knowledge (history) +12, Perception +6, Spellcraft +12, Stealth +6
**Languages** Abyssal, Aklo, Common, Draconic, Ignan, Infernal
**SQ** arcane bond (object)
**Combat Gear** potion of cure serious wounds, potion of resist fire 10; **Other Gear** masterwork dagger

## TELEPORTING TO THE EDGE OF OBLIVION

A short time later the PCs leave Bemmea and arrive at the observatory. Read or paraphrase the following.

*A bronze half-sphere tops a tall stone structure on a hill, its walls cracked from centuries of age. A complicated set of tubes and rods made of brass and glass protrude from the top of the bronze sphere. A large door opens at the base of the observatory. "It's about time you arrived," speaks a raspy voice. "I've been waiting all morning."*

The speaker is a thin man, hunched over and wearing a complicated set of lenses and crystals on a network of iron and leather bands around his forehead. He introduces himself impatiently as Glek, observer of the otherworldly. He watches for fallen stars, though he hasn't seen one for over five years. Glek takes the characters to a chamber within the sprawling observatory where lies a stone teleportation circle. There, speaking a few words of power, Glek opens up a gateway that blows hot wind through the room and reveals the standing stones at the edge of the Western Wastes.

## THE WESTERN WASTES

When the PCs arrive at the Western Wastes, read or paraphrase the following:

*Hot wind and dust howl through a set of standing stones looming thirty feet high, their surfaces scoured by the constant assault. Crumbling walls pierce out of the cracked earth of the wastes, the last remnants of towns and cities destroyed centuries earlier. The chime begins to hum, touching on the remnants of twisted ley lines now long dead.*

The characters can easily use the chime to triangulate the location of the Leystone. As they travel through the edge of the Western Wastes they might witness many strange sights including huge shambling forms far off in the distance. They might see strange arcane patterns form in the clouds above. They might stumble upon a storm of boneshard sleet, a gravity quake, or a storm that howls and whispers with the voices of the dead of the Great Mage Wars.

As they follow the continued humming of the ley line chime, they arrive two days later at the ruined Leystone.

## PART 2: THE LEYSTONE OF THE INDIGO STAR

As the PCs approach the Leystone, read the following:

*The dust of cracked mud blows past, revealing a spire of smooth black stone jutting out of the ground ahead. It rises over one hundred feet into the air like the tip of a knife. A great flood seems to have carved away the ravine wall and exposed the strange structure, which must have been buried in the earth for hundreds of years.*

A trapezoidal entryway blocked by a pair of heavy stone doors stands at the front of the structure. Stone carvings of stern tiefling faces mark the surface of each door, their pupil-less eyes staring out over the dead wastelands.

Much of the Leystone lies beneath the cracked earth, yet the upper spire of the Leystone and its entryway have been exposed over years of erosion.

A PC who succeeds at a DC 17 Perception check notices that the air feels much colder as one approaches the doors. A character succeeding at a DC 19 Knowledge (arcana) check learns that each door is infused with a powerful necrotic enchantment, requiring some sort of key to pass through safely.

Askalan originally found the key to this door when he learned about the Leystone itself. Not being the sharpest knife in the drawer, he buried the key nearby under a stack of flat stones. A character can see this stack of stones with a DC 17 Perception check. If they investigate the stack of stones, they find a black iron clawed gauntlet with a strange glyph on the palm. Under the glove is a parchment with the word "power" written on it in Infernal and a note in Common that says, "Find a better hiding spot."

The door opens for anyone who places their gloved hand on the door and speaks the word "power" in Infernal. Anyone attempting to open the door without wearing the glove and speaking the word takes 8d8 points of negative energy damage (DC 15 Fortitude save for half).

### 1. THE ENTRY HALL

When the PCs reach the entry hall, read or paraphrase the following.

*Scintillating colors shine against the flat-black walls of this hall. The left side of the wall looks as though it has melted. The petrified forms of tieflings reach out from the molten stone, their hands clawed and mouths agape in silent agony.*

*Three large circles have been carved into the floor of the hall, each circle containing a strange glyph. The first of these glyphs glows blue and the second glows violet. The third does not glow and large cracks from the molten walls to the left snake through it, splitting into three pieces. A gray liquid seeps out from the crack. Two doors line the left wall and a third door sits at the far right side of the hall.*

Characters who investigate the runes on the floor can attempt a DC 19 Knowledge (arcana) check. On a success, they are able to feel two distinct forms of energy coming from the glyphs. The blue energy feels like arcane cold energy while the violet rune radiates a strange astral energy not native to this world.

If a character moves within five feet of the dead glyph, the gray fluid spills out forming into two gray oozes with the giant creature template. The oozes also gain an additional slam attack.

The closest door on the left is protected with a *glyph of warding* cast by Askalan. If triggered, the glyph inflicts 5d8 points of lightning damage to the triggering creature and

all creatures within 5 feet of her. Askalan placed this glyph here using a password that died with him, so the glove will not disarm it.

## 2. ASKALAN'S STUDY

When the PCs enter this room, read or paraphrase the following:

*Piles of parchment lay scattered across the floor of this chamber. A large table sits on the far side of the room likewise piled with parchment. An arcane symbol has been drawn onto the floor in red chalk, and a carved statue of a stern female tiefling stands on the northern side of the room. A tangle of bedding lies in one corner among piles of candles melted down to pools of wax.*

This room, which had once served as the quarters for the commander of the Leystone, had become Askalan's study. Askalan's incomprehensible notes are scattered everywhere. A mixture of mathematical formulas and arcane scrawlings cover the walls, sometimes rubbed out or overwritten.

Characters who spend the time to investigate Askalan's notes learn the following:

- About five years ago, Askalan came upon a fallen star from the sky above. It glowed with tremendous power. He took it to his home on the outskirts of Bemmea.
- Askalan spent years studying the star, which had its own strange form of intelligence.
- Two years ago Askalan found this Leystone of Vael Turog, lost during the Mage Wars. It once held tremendous power but was dormant when Askalan encountered it.
- After a year of studying this structure, Askalan learned how to use the fallen star to act as the stone's power source. He placed the meteorite in a cell and the Leystone came to life.

Characters may dig deeper into Askalan's notes with a successful DC 18 Linguistics or DC 18 Knowledge (arcana) check. On a success, the character who performs the check learns the following additional pieces of information. Anyone who attempts this check and fails takes 3d6 points of damage as the pages project Askalan's madness into their minds.

- The power cell sends raw arcane energy into a pair of large brass cauldrons, where it mixes with a blue fluid. This fluid then goes into the central chamber, where its energy causes a huge black obelisk to spin rapidly and draw nearby dead ley lines to the Leystone.
- This spinning obelisk can use the Leystone's power to infuse magic into powerful magical artifacts, but the energy isn't entirely stable.
- Spheres of a black arcana-absorbing metal kept within a pair of control rooms can be placed in the large brass cauldrons. This draws arcane energy out of the pipelines and slows down the obelisk.
- Portions of the chamber were damaged hundreds of years ago when the entire Leystone stayed on in full power for too long. It melted the stone and killed many of the tieflings who worked within the Leystone.
- Askalan himself had to manually insert the arcana-absorbing spheres to reduce the speed of the obelisk or it might have destroyed the entire structure—though he then took the spheres out.
- Among the notes are two words written in Infernal. They are "Ignite" and "Infuse" and are used to open the doors in areas 4 and 8, respectively.

This chamber also contains a copy of Askalan's spellbook with the following spells: *mage hand, mending, chill touch, mage armor, shield, arcane lock, scorching ray, dispel magic, fireball, glyph of warding, magic circle against evil, nondetection, protection from energy, stoneskin, dismissal,* and *planar binding.*

## 3. THE CONTROL ROOM

When the PCs enter this room, read the following.

*A glyphed circle sits on the dark stone floor. Three large stone blocks cut into angles form a half-circle facing the door. Each of these three blocks contains three brass-lined basins of a strange metallic liquid. The leftmost block is badly cracked and the liquid within the bowls is darkly tinted.*

This room served as the primary monitoring room for the Leystone. When unused, all the basins have a still reflective metallic liquid within them. When one stands in the circle, however, one can call upon the liquid to form images of various rooms in the Leystone. Activating the basins requires a successful DC 19 Use Magic Device check. Failure on this check results in a powerful psychic feedback that inflicts 3d6 points of damage to the one attempting the check and anyone aiding them.

On a success, the character performing the check can observe six of the nine rooms of the Leystone: the entryway and chambers 2, 4, 5, 7, and 10. The block that controlled the pools to scry upon chambers 8 and 9, as well as the hallway between them, was broken when those rooms were damaged five centuries ago. Any character who attempts to activate those pools with a Use Magic Device check automatically fails the check and takes 3d6 points of damage. A successful DC 19 Knowledge (arcana) check reveals the danger of activating these pools.

## 4. THE COMPRESSION CHAMBER

When the PCs enter this room, read the following:

*A violet glow shines across the black stonework of this chamber. A pair of vented iron blocks, roughly ten feet on each side, hum and shake violently. A pair of twisting glass and metal tubes filled with a deep-blue liquid feed into the blocks from the eastern wall. Another glass tube filled with a glowing light-blue liquid feeds into the north wall. A black iron door with the stern face of a tiefling on its surface stands on the north side of the chamber.*

The large blocks of iron and stone in this chamber serve to compress the deep blue liquid into a form suitable to conduct the arcane energy coming out of the cell. The infused liquid then flows into the arcane dampener in room 5.

A spark (see *Midgard Bestiary*, page 87) has been living within the iron blocks, feeding off of the arcane residue that flows into the chamber. When the PCs enter the chamber, the spark breaks away from the blocks and attempts to inhabit an arcane spellcaster if possible. If unsuccessful, it attacks with its spells.

A character succeeding at a DC 12 Perception check notices necrotic energy flowing from the door. The door can be opened by a creature placing the glove found outside the Leystone upon it and speaking the word "Ignite".

Anyone attempting to open the door without using the glove and speaking the password takes 8d8 points of negative energy damage (DC 15 Fortitude save for half).

## 5. THE ARCANE DAMPENER

A pair of doors leads from room 4 to room 5, creating a buffer between the two rooms. One door must be closed before the other one will open.

When the PCs enter room 5, read the following:

*A large brass orb sits in the center of this room atop a black stone platform. Glass tubes filled with a glowing blue liquid run from the sphere to the eastern and southern walls. Another tube filled with a scintillating violet energy flows into the sphere from the northern wall.*

*The top of the sphere appears to be open and above it hangs a canister of brass and glass attached to a complicated network of metal supports. A black orb floats in the center of the canister. A panel of glyphed metal sits on the eastern wall.*

The metal panel controls the pillar, which can lower the canister into the brass sphere. A PC can use the panel with a successful DC 17 Use Magic Device check. Failure results in the pillar moving haphazardly, dropping in too quickly and emitting a burst of arcane energy. Any creature in the room when this occurs takes 8d6 points of electricity damage (DC 14 Reflex save for half).

When the canister drops in, the blue and violet light begins to fade, and the power being fed to the sphere in room 10 is lowered.

## 6. THE RUNOFF POOLS

When the PCs enter room 6, read the following:

*Two large pools of a glowing green liquid sit in the floor of the chamber, illuminating the melted stone around them. One of these has overflowed, and bolts of black lightning arc from the molten stone on the southern wall to the western pool of green liquid. Large pipes on the northern wall drip more of the green liquid into the pools.*

The green liquid in this chamber is a by-product of the arcane fluid flowing through the Leystone. It is filtered out by the brass sphere in room 7 and fed through these pipes into the pools.

Any living creature that touches a pool takes 4d8 points of acid damage and 4d8 points of lightning damage (DC 15 Fortitude save for half).

Arcane instability has created a malevolent pool of the liquid that forms into a black pudding that glows green instead of black. When a creature gets within 10 feet of the southwestern corner of the room, the pudding animates and attacks.

## 7. THE DAMAGED ARCANE DAMPENER

Unlike the doors leading to room 5, both doors leading to room 7 have been destroyed. When the characters enter room 7, read or summarize the following:

*The walls of this chamber have been warped beyond anything like the others in the Leystone. A tarnished bronze sphere sits on a cracked stone pillar in the center of the room. Three glass tubes feed into and lead out of the bronze sphere: one shining blue feeding into the south wall, one a brilliant violet coming in from the west, and one a dark thick green leading to the east. The top of the bronze sphere appears open, and bolts of energy spontaneously erupt from the sphere and arc into the nearby walls. Wreckage of twisted brass hangs from the ceiling and a glass canister capped by brass sits on the floor nearby. A sphere of perfect blackness sits in the center of the glass canister.*

Unlike room 5, this room is badly damaged. The glass canister must be placed into the brass sphere manually while simultaneously disrupting the arcing energy pouring out of the sphere. Doing so requires a successful DC 19 Sleight of Hand check by one PC and a successful DC 19 Use Magic Device check by another. Failure on either of these skill checks results in a blasting arc of arcane energy. Everyone within the room takes 8d6 points of electricity damage (DC 14 Reflex save for half).

When the canister is placed into the sphere, the violet and blue light dims. If both canisters are placed in both spheres in rooms 5 and 7, the energy pouring out of the arcane cell lowers considerably, the obelisk in room 9 begins to slow down, and the cell in room 10 can now be safely opened.

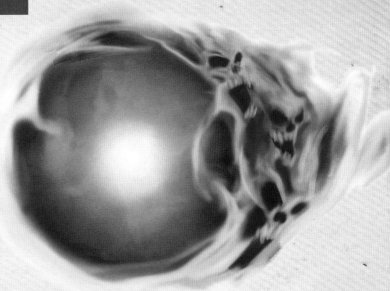

## 8. ENTRYWAY TO THE OBELISK

When the characters approach this hall, read or summarize the following:

*A pair of large doors stand at the western end of this T-shaped hall. A carved tiefling face stares out from each door, one male with its mouth open in a silent roar, and one female with eyes of brilliant sapphires. In many places, the smooth stone walls of these halls appear melted and almost organic. A single petrified hand reaches out from the molten stone, its fingers tipped in long claws. The walls and floor of this hall vibrate from some powerful but unseen force.*

These doors are heavily protected, requiring the glove to open as well as the password found in room 2. A character succeeding at a DC 19 Knowledge (arcana) check realizes both doors are protected with abjuration magic. When a living creature gets close to the doors, both doors say, "speak the word and enter" in Infernal. If a PC attempts to open the doors without speaking the proper word, or if he fails at a DC 21 Use Magic Device check to try to bypass the doors, the male door breathes out a blast of fire while bolts of lightning arc from the eyes of the female door. Those within 30 feet of the door take 10d6 points of fire damage and 10d6 points of electricity damage, requiring two separate DC 16 Reflex saves to take half damage from each source.

A character wearing the glove found outside of the Leystone can open the door by placing her gloved hand on the door and saying the word "Infuse" in Infernal.

## 9. THE CHAMBER OF THE OBELISK

When the PCs enter this room, read the following.

*A powerful wind roars around this vast chamber. The walls of the chamber angle inward as they soar to the full height of the Leystone's central spire one hundred feet above. A huge black obelisk floats and spins in the center of the chamber so quickly that its sharp edges blur. A large shadow swirls around the top of the obelisk far above.*

*Below the spinning obelisk sits a circular shining metal table on a large circular dais, its edges marked with carefully etched glyphs. Two large glass tubes of shining blue liquid feed into the bottom of the circular dais.*

This large obelisk is the primary force that draws ley lines to the Leystone. It acts as a conductor for that power and channels it into the metal table. Every few minutes a bolt of brilliant violet energy arcs from the bottom tip of the obelisk to the top of the table. Anyone who gets in the way of that arc takes 10d6 + 40 points of force damage. If this damage kills the creature, it is disintegrated. This damage can be negated with a successful DC 18 Reflex save.

A PC succeeding on a DC 19 Knowledge (arcana) check realizes the obelisk is spinning too fast to draw any sort of stable magic. In fact, if the power of the Leystone is not reduced within the next few weeks, the obelisk will lose its stability and explode, destroying the Leystone and everything around it.

The power of the obelisk has drawn a very young void dragon named Ixaranum, who feeds off of the escalating energy of the obelisk. Currently, Ixaranum swirls around the top of the obelisk in a shadowy form. A PC succeeding on a DC 21 Knowledge (arcana) check realizes the shadow swirling above the obelisk is sentient; if the PC exceeds the DC by 5 or more, she knows the creature is a young—but powerful—void dragon.

If the PCs have successfully removed the Indigo Star from the arcane cell in room 10, the dragon drops down onto the floor of the chamber and demands they give the Star over to it. If they agree, it devours the Star, roars in ecstasy, and returns to its home in the void.

If they fight Ixaranum, the dragon begins the battle by using its breath weapon. If the PCs have brought the Indigo Star with them, it stands in the way and absorbs the energy of the breath weapon. It's obvious that this will destroy the Star; one of the PCs can push the Star out of the way and take on the full breath weapon herself. Otherwise, the Star is destroyed by the attack but absorbs Ixaranum's breath weapon damage completely. The dragon decides to use dimension door as its next action regardless of the outcome.

---

| VERY YOUNG VOID DRAGON | CR 16 |
|---|---|

**XP 76,800**

CN Large dragon

**Init** +10; **Senses** dragon senses; Perception +29

### DEFENSE

**AC** 30, touch 25, flat-footed 24 (+10 deflection, +6 Dex, +5 natural, −1 size)

**hp** 237 (19d12+114)

**Fort** +17, **Ref** +17, **Will** +14

**DR** 5/magic; **Immune** cold, paralysis, sleep; **SR** 27

### OFFENSE

**Speed** 50 ft., fly 200 ft. (good)

**Melee** bite +27 (2d6+12 plus 1d6 cold), 2 claws +26 (1d8+8 plus 1d6 cold), tail slap +21 (1d8+4), 2 wings +21 (1d6+4)

**Space** 10 ft.; Reach 5 ft.

**Special Attacks** breath weapon (40-ft. cone, 8d10 cold, DC 25), cold of the void, redirect ranged attack

**Spell-Like Abilities** (CL 19th; concentration +24)

At will—*dimension door*

**Sorcerer Spells Known** (CL 5th; concentration +10)

2nd (5/day)—*darkness, starbolt*DM (DC 17)

1st (8/day)—*ray of the eclipse*DM, *shadow hands*DM (DC 16), *stumble gap*APG (DC 16), *voidmote*DM (DC 16)

0 (at will)—*arcane mark, deepen shadow*DM, *detect magic, hide*DM, *shadow bite*DM (DC 15), *touch of fatigue* (DC 15)

### STATISTICS

**Str** 26, **Dex** 22, **Con** 23, **Int** 13, **Wis** 16, **Cha** 21

**Base Atk** +19; **CMB** +28; **CMD** 54 (58 vs. trip)

**Feats** Alertness, Combat Expertise, Dimensional AgilityUC, Dimensional AssaultUC, Dimensional DervishUC, Dimensional SavantUC, Hover, Improved Initiative, Skill Focus (Stealth), Weapon Focus (bite)

**Skills** Acrobatics +6 (+14 to jump), Bluff +25, Fly +17, Intimidate +25, Knowledge (arcana) +23, Knowledge (geography) +23, Perception +29, Sense Motive +29, Stealth +28

**Languages** Aklo, Draconic

**SQ** no breath

---

## 10. THE CHAMBER OF THE ARCANE CELL

When the characters enter this room, read or paraphrase the following:

*Violet light shines across the black stone of this chamber. A glass-encased sphere held by a metal scaffold swirls with violet energy. Large glass tubes filled with the same violet energy emerge from the brass enclosure and flow into the walls south and east. A large iron vent sits in the center of the floor.*

*As you stand in front of the orb, the silhouette of a hand presses up against the inside of the glass, four long fingers reaching out for escape from the torment within.*

If the characters have not yet placed the arcane dampeners into the brass spheres, they can sense tremendous energy still flows out from the sphere and through the tubes. It is clear any attempt to break into the sphere will meet with catastrophic results and destroy the entire complex and anything within it. The power feeding out of the cell must be lowered before it can be opened.

If the arcane dampeners are in place in rooms 5 and 7, the arcane energy isn't nearly as dangerous and the sphere can be cracked open. A purple liquid bursts out from the sphere and flows into the vent on the floor. The Indigo Star falls to the ground and pushes itself up.

The Indigo Star appears to be a child of five years. Its head is hairless, its skin pale, and its limbs seem longer than they should be. Its eyes shine with violet light. The Indigo Star does not speak any language known to the characters but will follow their instructions.

The PCs have a few choices in this chamber. They might choose not to crack the sphere at all and leave the structure as it is. If they do so, the structure will explode as they make their way back across the Western Wastes. Instead, they might choose to bring the Indigo Star back to the Magocracy of Bemmea or perhaps slay the Star here. Slaying the Star causes no catastrophe, but the Star's luminescent blood flows from its body into the vent, forever losing its arcane luster.

If the PCs bring the Star back out with them to chamber 9, Ixaranum demands they let it devour the Star.

At the end of the adventure, if the PCs treat the Indigo Star well, it pierces into its own chest and draws forth a glowing violet stone. It then hands this stone to the PC who treated it best. This stone acts as a luckstone. Otherwise the luckstone is left over after the Star's death.

## CONCLUSION

This adventure can conclude in a few different ways, all centering around the choices the characters make in relation to the Indigo Star. The characters might decide to set the Star free to wander into the Western Wastes, a choice that likely will not kill the Star but might have other unseen consequences. They might choose to sacrifice the Star to Ixaranum. They might choose to destroy the Star themselves, fearing the power it contains. They might choose to bring the Star along with them, hiding it from the Magocracy of Bemmea, which can lead to many future adventures. Or they might simply choose to bring the Star back to the Magocracy as instructed. None of these choices are wrong and each choice has the potential to lead to future fantastic adventures.

# PALACE OF THE WIND LORDS

An adventure for 5 7th-level PCs set in a flying city in the Southlands

*by James J. Haeck*

## GM INTRODUCTION

An ancient palace constructed by the mighty Wind Lord Boreas has a new master: the sorcerous gnoll matriarch Odjanbago and her clan—the Archthieves. With the flying Sky Palace at her command, Odjanbago's legendary clan of thieves and killers have cast a shadow of fear over the Southlands' northwestern desert. All tremble in fear of the Archthieves, from the jinnborn tribes of the Dominion of the Wind Lords to the priests of Bastet in Nuria Natal. Even lords of Midgard's Seven Cities grow uneasy at their mention. Whether they hail from the Southlands or elsewhere in Midgard, the PCs must shoulder the responsibility of ending Odjanbago's reign of terror.

## SUMMARY

The Palace of the Wind Lords, also known as the Sky Palace, was once a retreat for Boreas the North Wind. When Boreas betrayed the Wind Lords and departed for the Northlands, the magic that supported the palace began to fade, and the city that once surrounded the palace has been dashed upon the earth below. When Odjanbago and her gnolls discovered the flying fortress, only the central palace remained. Odjanbago battled the palace's last owner, a djinni named Leyla, and trapped her within a magic crystal.

No matter the PCs' reasons for entering the Sky Palace, an army of gnolls, demons, and evil witches stands between them and victory.

## FACTIONS

The following groups and individuals play an important role in this adventure.

**Aechatta.** This elemental gearforged was once a free air spirit before being bound by humans to a physical form. He led a party of adventurers in an attack on the Sky Palace about one week ago, but their raid ended disastrously. With his metal body in ruins, Aechatta simply wishes to gain the power to emancipate his spirit and return to the Plane of Air.

**Gnoll Archthieves.** Odjanbago, Archthief matriarch, uses the power of her captured djinni to slake her thirst for power and stroke her massive ego. Her gnolls aid her out of abject fear, not loyalty—though the promise of fabulous wealth also keeps them in line.

**Leyla.** Leyla is completely at Odjanbago's mercy. She has no will of her own, but she hates the gnolls with every fiber of her elemental being. Even death would be a welcome escape from servitude. Djinn are predisposed to twisting the intentions of their masters' wishes, but Leyla considers herself bound to honestly serve anyone who rescues her from this torment.

## ADVENTURE HOOKS

As your players' GM, you know best how to involve the PCs in this adventure. The following adventure hooks are provided to inspire and assist you.

- **Theft.** Baron Raúl Cazagoza of Capleon has been robbed! The extravagantly wealthy lord of Capleon—one of Midgard's Seven Cities—paid handsomely for an ivory-white Mharoti camel, believing that the beautiful beast possessed magical powers. Not long after the money and the camel changed hands, the Archthieves and the Sky Palace descended upon the baron's caravan and stole his prize. He sent a team of mercenaries to reclaim it, but they never returned. He is willing to pay a king's ransom to retrieve the white camel.

- **Hunting the North Wind.** The ascended Wind Lord Boreas was exiled from the Dominion of the Wind Lords and was reborn as a dark god in the northern tundras of Midgard. Adventurers from both Midgard and the Southlands have reason to want Boreas's power diminished, as he often visits his ancient home in Southlands to wage war against the other Wind Lords and their followers. Rumor has it a *blade of the south wind*, a weapon fashioned to slay the North Wind, was locked within the Sky Palace after Boreas's fled the Southlands.

- **Three Wishes?** A popular rumor says the fearsome Archthieves have been able to terrorize the Middle Sea region with impunity because they have a djinni in their service. If the PCs have need of a wish, an ally may know where they can find one.

# ADVENTURE START

The PCs approach the palace by its tether, an anchor currently weighed atop a sandy bluff overlooking a murky lake. The trek up the hill is simple enough, but the sphere of whirling air keeping the Sky Palace aloft creates vicious sandstorms around its mooring.

**Sandstorms.** Any outdoor area within half a mile of the palace, including bridges between palace rooms, is scoured by sandstorms. A sandstorm reduces visibility to 1d10 x 5 feet and gives a –4 penalty on Perception checks. It deals 1d4 points of nonlethal damage per hour to any creatures caught in the open.

**Falling.** The Sky Palace is floating 100 feet above a small lake. If a creature falls from the palace, it may make a DC 18 Reflex saving throw to twist toward the lake. A creature that falls in the water takes half the usual falling damage.

**Clearance.** Rooms within the Palace of the Wind Lords are 100 feet tall unless stated otherwise, and the hallways between rooms are little more than rail-less bridges exposed to the elements. Doors are 40 feet tall and 20 feet wide. Huge or smaller creatures must succeed at a DC 15 Strength check to open or close a door, though all interior doors are left open enough for one Medium creature to pass through at a time. The palace was clearly constructed for a massive being, perhaps Boreas himself.

## 1. CLIFFSIDE MOORING

*You push through the howling sandstorm to the top of a rocky bluff. Above you looms the silhouette of a flying palace; a magnificent ruin of crumbling walls and broken battlements, surrounded by a perfect sphere of howling wind. At the top of this cliff is an anchor the size of a bull, linked by a sturdy chain to the citadel hovering above.*

Before the Sky Palace dropped anchor here, this cliff overlooked a gentle oasis 50 feet below. Another 50 feet above the cliff is the palace itself. Creatures cannot easily fly within the sandstorm that surrounds the palace, but may climb the anchor's chain (DC 17 Climb check).

## 2. CRUMBLING GATE

*At the top of the palace's mooring is an arched gateway tall enough to fit a savannah giraffe with room to spare. Its monumental doors are shut; engraved into their crumbling, cloudy-white stones are hundreds of djinn and winged soldiers, their scimitars drawn and their faces leering down. The lower engravings have been crudely altered to depict cackling, hyena-headed gnolls instead.*

A character who examines the doors can attempt a DC 17 Perception check to discover that the door is very slightly ajar, just enough to fit a crowbar or another small tool into the gap.

Attempting to force open the massive doors requires 1 minute of work and a successful DC 20 Strength check; creatures attempting the check without a crowbar or similar tool take a –4 penalty. Failure by 5 or more on this check alerts the gnoll gatekeepers inside, giving them time to retrieve the *horn of alarum* and hide behind the statue of Boreas (see Area 3).

## 3. GRAND GATEHOUSE

*Beyond the Sky Palace's enormous threshold is a gatehouse dominated by the towering statue of a winged old man, his long hair and shaggy beard blown in all directions by a wild gale. While the gatehouse and its furnishings are made of the same cloudy stone as the gates, the statue is carved from solid, unmelting ice. A cold wind surrounds the statue. There are doors to the northeast and northwest.*

If the PCs infiltrated the palace without alerting the gnolls within (see Area 2), add the following:

*Four mangy, hyena-headed humanoids bark and cackle at one another, squabbling over a zebra haunch in front of the statue. On the floor near them is an ivory bugle, forgotten in the scuffle.*

The four advanced gnolls in the gatehouse have abandoned their guard duties to fight over rations. They dropped their *horn of alarum* (see below) halfway between the base of the statue and the main gate. The gnolls take a –4 penalty on their Perception checks for the next 2 rounds while they squabble.

**Alert.** If the gnolls discover the PCs, one scraggly whelp remembers his orders and rushes to grab the horn of alarum and blow it (requiring a move action and then a standard action) to alert Odjanbago to the intrusion. If the matriarch is alerted to the PCs presence, two invisible stalkers uncoil from the icy statue of Boreas and wait until the PCs have let their guard down to ambush the most vulnerable character.

After the horn is blown, Odjanbago uses scrolls of sending to alert the gnolls in Areas 4 and 9, and the sand hag in Area 5 to prepare for intruders.

---

## HORN OF ALARUM

**Aura** faint abjuration; **CL** 1st
**Slot** none; **Price** 1,000 gp; **Weight** 2 lbs.

### DESCRIPTION

This ivory horn is decorated with engravings of trumpeting elephants. It produces no sound when blown, but instantly alerts the horn's owner of the direction of the creature that blew the horn as long as that creature is on the same plane of existence.

### CONSTRUCTION

**Requirements** Craft Wondrous Item, *alarm*; **Cost** 500 gp

## 4. DINING HALL AND THE SHIPWRECK

*This chamber is filled with the wreckage of what was once a lavish dining hall. Dishes of all shapes and sizes litter the room—some human-sized, others the size of humans! The devastation seems to have been caused by the single-masted ship that smashed through the chamber's walls. The wrecked ship takes up most of the room, and its hull is torn open. The sound of cackling gnolls echoes from inside the ship, and you see a trio of gnolls outside the ship, tossing around a metal leg. You can see the sandstorm raging outside the smashed walls, but it does not enter inside the palace walls.*

About a week ago, a wooden ship named the *Reddenwick* was caught in the Sky Palace's sphere of wind and plucked from the waters of the sea that separates Midgard and the Southlands. The lifted vessel smashed into the walls of the dining hall and is now lodged here with its belly torn open. Three gnoll berserkers are playing a game of toss-and-catch with a dismembered gearforged leg outside the ship.

Inside the *Reddenwick* are four gnolls: three bandit captains led by a musclebound gladiator named Gurzinbago, the Archthieves' second-in-command and prideful sister of matriarch Odjanbago. Gurzinbago wields a *+1 flail*. The gnolls are in the main hold ship, searching through the cargo and filling their pockets with gold taken from the slaughtered crew. Baron Raúl Cazagoza's stolen white camel is inside this ship (see "Aechatta," below), and the gnolls are here to return it to Odjanbago. Eight human corpses can be found throughout the ship, plus the legless body of a gearforged named Aechatta.

### GNOLL BANDIT CAPTAIN (3)     CR 3

**XP 800 each**
Gnoll fighter 2
CE Medium humanoid (gnoll)
**Init** +6; **Senses** darkvision 60 ft.; Perception +0

**DEFENSE**

**AC** 17, touch 13, flat-footed 14 (+3 armor, +2 Dex, +1 dodge, +1 natural)
**hp** 34 (4 HD; 2d8+2d10+14)
**Fort** +9, **Ref** +2, **Will** +0; +1 vs. fear

**OFFENSE**

**Speed** 30 ft.
**Melee** mwk scimitar +8 (1d6+4/18–20)

**STATISTICS**

**Str** 16, **Dex** 14, **Con** 16, **Int** 10, **Wis** 10, **Cha** 6
**Base Atk** +3; **CMB** +6; **CMD** 19
**Feats** Dodge, Improved Initiative, Power Attack, Weapon Focus (scimitar)
**Skills** Acrobatics +6, Intimidate +5
**Languages** Gnoll
**Other Gear** mwk studded leather, mwk scimitar

### GURZINBAGO     CR 6

**XP 2,400**
Gnoll fighter 5
CE Medium humanoid (gnoll)
**Init** +6; **Senses** darkvision 60 ft.; Perception –1

**DEFENSE**

**AC** 19, touch 12, flat-footed 17 (+6 armor, +2 Dex, +1 natural)
**hp** 62 (7 HD; 2d8+5d10+26)
**Fort** +9, **Ref** +3, **Will** +0; +1 vs. fear

**OFFENSE**

**Speed** 30 ft.
**Melee** *+1 heavy flail* +13/+8 (1d10+10/19–20)
**Special Attacks** weapon training (flails +1)

**STATISTICS**

**Str** 19, **Dex** 14, **Con** 14, **Int** 8, **Wis** 8, **Cha** 10
**Base Atk** +6; **CMB** +10; **CMD** 22
**Feats** Dazzling Display, Improved Initiative, Intimidating Prowess, Power Attack, Toughness, Weapon Focus (heavy flail), Weapon Specialization (heavy flail)

BRYAN SYME

**Skills** Acrobatics +2, Intimidate +11
**Languages** Gnoll
**SQ** armor training 1
**Other Gear** breastplate, +1 heavy flail

**Aechatta.** This air elemental gearforged was the leader of the first adventuring party hired to reclaim Baron Cazagoza's prized camel and captain of the *Reddenwick*. His legs were torn off by the Archthieves when they slaughtered his crew, and has been feigning death ever since. If the gnolls are killed or otherwise eliminated, he stops feigning death and tries to get the party to help him: he accepted Cazagoza's offer to rescue the camel for an ulterior reason. Aechatta is an elemental gearforged—an air elemental spirit unwillingly bound to a mechanical body. He seeks the djinni Leyla, fabled master of the Palace of the Wind Lords, in the hopes she can return his spirit to the Plane of Air. Without his legs, he can do little to help, but he begs dearly for the PCs' aid. Aechatta's stats are not included in this adventure, since he will not be able to help them.

**Treasure.** The gnolls are laden with 150 gp in coins and semiprecious gems.

## 5. GARDEN OF SALT AND STONE

*A cloud of whirling sand engulfs this open courtyard. Through the sandstorm, you catch a glimpse of three tall standing stones in the southeast. The wind whistles through holes in the stones, and it sings a quiet, despairing melody.*

Also read the following if the *horn of alarum* was blown.

*You briefly see the delicate figure of a young woman chained between the standing stones. She turns to face you and you briefly see her tear-streaked face before she is engulfed by the sands.*

Read the following instead if the *horn of alarum* was not blown.

*You see a cloaked figure with wispy white hair in the east of the room. It turns to face you and you can just barely see its withered face before it vanishes into the sandstorm.*

This aged creature is a vile sand hag (see *Southlands Bestiary*, page 83) named Mambinn. If the *horn of alarum* alerted Odjanbago, then the hag already disguised herself as the djinni Leyla, bound in chains by her wrists and ankles to three standing stones. If not, she assumes her disguise as soon as the sandstorm conceals her, appearing as a beautiful woman with icy blue skin barely visible through her spiral-patterned headscarf.

The open-air garden was once green and filled with tall cedar trees, sweet myrrh, and flowering saffron. Since Leyla's capture, it has become a sand-blasted plain of worn stones and withered plants. The sandstorm here restricts visibility to 30 feet to creatures without blindsight in addition to its other effects. In the west of the room is Leyla's boudoir, but a sizeable chasm was created near the bedroom when the *Reddenwick* crashed into the palace. A creature who unwittingly steps into the chasm must succeed at a DC 25 Reflex save or fall 100 feet to the water below.

**Mambinn's Deception.** The sand hag Mambinn joined the Archthieves for the chance to spread chaos and misery on a massive scale, and her approach to intruders is no different. Pretending to be the benevolent Leyla, she promises to grant her rescuers three wishes each if they free her from her enchanted chains. She claims the "magical key" is in her boudoir, lying through false tears. She urges the PCs to watch out for the crevasse between her and the bedroom, but uses a "*move earth*" spell to close it up—in reality a *hallucinatory terrain* spell designed to look like part of the crevasse is closed up.

Mambinn's chains are a *minor image*. Trying to break them or unlock them with the key from the boudoir instantly reveals the deception. When found out, Mambinn calls six anubians (see *Southlands Bestiary*, page 9) from the sand while she uses *invisibility* and flees, hoping to ambush the PCs in another room of the GM's choice.

## 6. LEYLA'S BOUDOIR

The djinni's boudoir has all the trappings of a lavish bedroom, but the beautiful portraits, quilted bedsheets, and silk nightgowns are ragged and torn. Despite the squalor, the walls shine with all colors of the rainbow, glinting as the light shifts. A character investigating the walls who succeeds at a DC 19 Perception check notices that the mirror-like walls are actually coated with motionless prismatic beetles. A character succeeding at a DC 20 Perception check finds a silver key hidden in a shredded portrait of Leyla. Touching the key causes the entire room to explode in a flurry of wings and flashing light as two prismatic beetle swarms (see Southlands Bestiary, page 79) surge from the walls to devour the nearest living creature.

**Treasure.** Looting Leyla's chamber yields four sapphires each worth 100 gp and one ethereal robe that glows like silver, moonlit fog. It is nonmagical, but worth 1,000 gp.

## 7. PILLARS OF SALT

*The air here is still and stagnant, and it tastes of salt. Even the roaring wind just outside sounds muted and distant. In the north is a fifty-foot-tall ice statue of Boreas, looming godlike over twenty perfectly white petrified worshipers.*

Two salt devils (see *Southlands Bestiary*, page 37) lurk at the base of the statue. They are bound to follow Odjanbago's orders; if the *horn of alarum* was blown previously, the gnoll matriarch ordered these devils to kill all non-gnoll intruders. If the horn was not blown, they cannot attack unless the PCs strike first. They sarcastically mock the PCs, hoping to goad them into violence.

**Worshipers.** At the height of Boreas's power, he commanded a cult of thousands. The two dozen petrified worshipers here were transformed into pillars of salt, smote in the midst of prayer by a higher power when Boreas departed for the Northlands. A pillar disintegrates into fine grains when touched, and the creature that touched it is cursed by a *bestow curse* effect of the GM's choice (DC 14 Will save negates).

**Grand Door.** The ornate stone doorway to the throne room (Area 10) can only be opened by a powerful gust of wind, such as the *gust of wind* spell or an attack from the *blade of the south wind* in Area 7.

## 8. HOUSE OF MYSTIC CRYSTAL

*The air is charged with the ineffable sensation of magic. A twenty-foot-tall sky-blue crystal hums with energy in the center of the room, and its surface crawls with turquoise insects. In its center is the silver hilt of a sword with no blade. Several bookshelves have been forcefully knocked to the ground and dozens of books and scrolls are strewn across the sandy floor. Three colorful carpets are rolled up tightly in the southeast of the room.*

The insects crawling on the storm crystal are three manabane scarab swarms (see *Southlands Bestiary*, page 65), which are feeding on the crystal's magic. Inside the crystal is the hilt of a *blade of the south wind* (see below). The crystal weighs 4,000 pounds, has AC 5, has 100 hit points, and has immunity to all damage except bludgeoning damage from magical weapons.

**Magic Carpets.** The three rugs in the room seem to be carpets of flying when identified, but they actually fly their riders into the nearest obstacle, dealing falling damage for the distance they travel to reach the obstacle.

### BLADE OF THE SOUTH WIND

**Aura** faint evocation; **CL** 3rd
**Slot** none; **Price** 2,975 gp; **Weight** 2 lbs.
**DESCRIPTION**

This silver hilt has no blade and deals 1d4 points of bludgeoning damage when used as a melee weapon. By speaking a command word, the wielder summons a greatsword-sized blade of wind from the hilt. The sword acts as a *+1 greatsword* but is light enough to be wielded in one hand. Summoning and dispelling the blade is a swift action. Once per day as a standard action, the wielder can unleash a *gust of wind* from the blade.

**CONSTRUCTION**

**Requirements** Craft Magic Arms and Armor, *gust of wind*, *summon blade*^DM; **Cost** 1,675 gp

## 9. ARCHTHIEF BARRACKS

*This barracks is thick with the scent of blood, carrion, and wet dog. Seven hastily-constructed wooden bunks are lined against one of the walls. The floor is strewn with gnawed-clean bones, and a group of armored gnolls are batting them around like toys.*

This structure is divided into two rooms—Areas 8 and 9. If a battle takes place in one room, the occupants of the other hear it.

Twelve gnolls and two gnoll bandit captains (see Area 4) make these barracks their home and are so fearful of their matriarch that they never leave unless ordered. At any given time, six gnolls and one gnoll bandit captain are awake and playing, gambling, or fighting. The rest are in their bunks and awaken if combat breaks out in Area 8 or 9 (or are already awake if the *horn of alarum* was blown within the past hour).

**Treasure.** Beneath each of the seven bunks is a small chest containing 3d6 gp and a *potion of cure serious wounds*.

## 10. WINDBORNE ARMORY

*The distinctive scent of myrrh and patchouli hangs heavy in the air. A single talisman-draped gnoll sits cross-legged amidst a heap of swords and daggers, a smoking censer in his lap. Around the gnoll are racks of spears and blades and suits of metal and hide armor.*

This structure is divided into two rooms—Areas 8 and 9. If a battle takes place in one room, the occupants of the other room hear it.

Smoke emanates from a cult fanatic's *censer of conjuring air elementals*, which has the following additional property:

If the wielder concentrates when using the censer, he can animate up to 5 unattended weapons as flying swords that act on his initiative. If he ceases concentrating, the weapons fall inert at the end of his turn.

The *censer* loses the ability to animate swords for anyone other than the gnoll.

65

## GNOLL CULT FANATIC — CR 5

**XP 1,600**

Gnoll cleric 5

CE Medium humanoid (gnoll)

**Init** +1; **Senses** darkvision 60 ft.; Perception +2

### DEFENSE

**AC** 17, touch 12, flat-footed 16 (+4 armor, +1 deflection, +1 Dex, +1 natural)

**hp** 57 (7d8+26)

**Fort** +9, **Ref** +2, **Will** +6

### OFFENSE

**Speed** 30 ft.

**Melee** dagger +5 (1d4+1/19–20)

**Special Attacks** channel negative energy 6/day (DC 15, 3d6)

**Domain Spell-Like Abilities** (CL 5th; concentration +7)

  5/day—*lightning arc* (1d6+2 electricity), *touch of evil* (2 rounds)

**Cleric Spells Prepared** (CL 5th; concentration +7)

  3rd—*bestow curse* (DC 15), *gaseous form*ᴰ

  2nd—*align weapon*ᴰ (evil only), *hold person* (2, DC 14), *spiritual weapon*

  1st—*bane* (DC 13), *command* (2, DC 13), *protection from good*ᴰ, *shield of faith*

  0 (at will)—*bleed* (DC 12), *detect magic*, *light*, *spark*ᴬᴾᴳ (DC 12)

  ᴰ Domain spell: **Domains** Air, Evil

### STATISTICS

**Str** 12, **Dex** 12, **Con** 14, **Int** 8, **Wis** 15, **Cha** 12

**Base Atk** +4; **CMB** +5; **CMD** 17

**Feats** Combat Casting, Extra Channel, Improved Channel, Toughness

**Skills** Bluff +4, Diplomacy +6, Knowledge (religion) +4

**Languages** Gnoll

**Other Gear** *+1 studded leather*, dagger, *ring of protection +1*

## FLYING SWORD (5) — CR 4

**XP 1,200**

Animated object

N Medium construct

**Init** +0; **Senses** darkvision 60 ft., low-light vision; Perception –5

### DEFENSE

**AC** 16, touch 10, flat-footed 16 (+6 natural)

**hp** 36 (3d10+20)

**Fort** +1, **Ref** +1, **Will** –4

**Defensive Abilities** hardness 10; **Immune** construct traits

### OFFENSE

**Speed** 30 ft., fly 30 ft. (clumsy)

**Melee** 2 slams +5 (1d6+2)

### STATISTICS

**Str** 14, **Dex** 10, **Con** —, **Int** —, **Wis** 1, **Cha** 1

**Base Atk** +3; **CMB** +5; **CMD** 15

**Skills** Fly –8

**SQ** animated object construction points

---

## 11. THRONE OF THE ARCHTHIEF

*A throne fit for a god towers before you. A mortal-sized staircase leads to the seat of the throne and a smaller throne has been constructed on the seat of the larger. On this throne sits a gnoll of incredible size—nearly ten feet tall—covered in scars, war paint, and ruby beads. In her lap is an orb of sky-blue crystal.*

If the PCs are detected when they enter, read the following.

*The gnoll stands, still holding the crystal orb, and howls with laughter. "E' cannit believe yer still alivin'!" she shrieks gleefully. "Your eyes see Odjanbago, Archthief! Tha master a' tha djinni's crystal! Ya grovel, now!"*

Odjanbago lusts for domination. Even false groveling appeases her and makes her willing to negotiate. Conversely, any hesitance or opposition from the PCs instantly drives her to anger. She holds the crystal aloft and uses her action to bark, "Djinni. Last wish. Give your life to kill tha intruders."

A deep crack appears on the side of the crystal, and a cloud of rotting wind (see *Southlands Bestiary*, page 82) seeps out of the crystal as the captured djinni Leyla begins to die. Every 2 rounds on initiative count 20, another rotting wind emerges from the crystal. After the third rotting wind is created, the crystal shatters and Leyla dies. Only touching the crystal—thereby becoming its new master—and wishing to save the djinni's life can prevent her death. A character succeeding at a DC 20 Knowledge (planes) check realizes this fact.

## ODJANBAGO — CR 9

**XP 6,400**

Gnoll evoker 9

CE Medium humanoid (gnoll)

**Init** +4; **Senses** darkvision 60 ft.; Perception +12

### DEFENSE

**AC** 13, touch 10, flat-footed 13 (+3 natural)

**hp** 93 (11 HD; 9d6+2d8+53)

**Fort** +9, **Ref** +3, **Will** +7

### OFFENSE

**Speed** 30 ft.

**Melee** mwk dagger +7 (1d4+1/19-20)

**Special Attacks** intense spells (+4 damage)

**Arcane School Spell-Like Abilities** (CL 9th; concentration +12)

  At will—*elemental wall* (9 rounds/day)

  6/day—*force missile* (1d4+4)

**Evoker Spells Prepared** (CL 9th; concentration +12)

  5th—*cone of cold* (2, DC 21)

  4th—*ice storm* (2), *resilient sphere* (DC 19)

  3rd—*fireball* (2, DC 19), *ray of exhaustion* (2, DC 16), *slow* (DC 16)

  2nd—*acid arrow*, *elemental surge*ᴰᴹ (2, DC 15), *glitterdust* (DC 15), *scorching ray* (2)

1st—*burning hands* (DC 17), *mage armor, magic missile* (3), *shield*

0 (at will)—*acid splash, light, mage hand, prestidigitation*

**Opposition Schools** enchantment, illusion

### STATISTICS

**Str** 12, **Dex** 10, **Con** 16, **Int** 16, **Wis** 12, **Cha** 10

**Base Atk** +5; **CMB** +6; **CMD** 16

**Feats** Craft Wondrous Item, Elemental Focus[APG] (cold), Elemental Focus[APG] (fire), Greater Spell Focus (evocation), Improved Initiative, Scribe Scroll, Spell Focus (evocation), Toughness

**Skills** Intimidate +11, Knowledge (arcana) +17, Knowledge (history) +17, Perception +12, Spellcraft +17

**Languages** Auran, Common, Gnoll, Ignan

**SQ** arcane bond (*amulet of natural armor +2*)

**Combat Gear** *potion of cure serious wounds, potion of resist fire 10*; **Other Gear** mwk dagger, *amulet of natural armor +2, headband of vast intelligence +2*

## CONCLUSION

If the PCs save Leyla, she grants them three wishes total (as per the *wish* spell), though one wish was already used to save her life. (She apologizes, but "it's an Unbreakable Law.") She begs them also to set her free so that she can return the Sky Palace to its former glory, potentially leaving only a single wish left for altruistic PCs. If the PCs spend their last wish on freeing Aechatta as well, Leyla is stunned by their selflessness and offers to serve

them willingly for a year and a day. Leyla's power has been diminished by her recent brush with death, so she must turn down wishes the GM considers beyond her power.

**Continuing the Adventure.** If the PCs want to claim the Sky Palace itself as their prize, they must spend one of their wishes to give one character mental control over the palace, just as Odjanbago did. If the PCs intend on returning Baron Raúl Cazagoza's prized white camel, it may just be an albino beast. On the other hand, what would happen on the return journey were the camel truly imbued with supernatural power?

# THE UNDYING TOURNAMENT

An adventure for five 8th-level PCs set in a subterranean city of the Ghouls

*by James J. Haeck*

## GM INTRODUCTION

Within the darakhul city of Gonderif, at the nadir of a thousand-foot-deep chasm, is the site of a vile tournament where Gonderif's most rebellious slaves and war prisoners are forced to fight to the death—and through undeath after undeath—until only one living champion remains. Whether they came as captives or as liberators, the PCs must survive the Undying Tournament.

## SUMMARY

The slaves of Gonderif outnumber their ghoulish masters ten to one. Any slaves brave enough to attempt to lead a rebellion are sent to the Undying Tournament, where they are "mercifully" promised freedom from slavery if they are the last prisoner standing. No one trusts this promise, but the insidious seed of hope for freedom is nonetheless planted in their hearts.

Depending on how PCs come to Gonderif's slave pits, they may or may not be forced to fight in the Undying Tournament; if they avoid detection, the tournament may not occur at all. Slaves and captives of many different races exist in the pits, and clever PCs may be able to overcome the racial tensions between the factions and unify a revolt against their undead jailers.

## FACTIONS

The following groups and individuals play an important role in this adventure.

**Corpse Tearers**. Both Gonderif and the Undying Tournament grounds are protected by the Corpse Tearers, one of the darakhul Imperial Legions. The Corpse Tearers have a reputation for being easily incensed and gained their name because of the frequent honor duels between members of the legion. PCs looking to distract legion forces in Gonderif could try to incite chaos among their ranks. All darakhul (see *Midgard Bestiary*, page 28) in this adventure belong to the legion and wear mithral scale mail (improving their AC to 24, flat-footed 20).

**Slaves**. The tournament grounds are home to nine of Gonderif's most headstrong and rebellious slaves, five of whom are detailed below. PCs will probably not become close with all of them, and you should choose several that interest you as a GM to serve in prominent roles in the adventure. All are bound by *rare spellbinding shackles* (see Area 1).

- **Alejandra chaotic good human**. A grandmother, ex-field sergeant, and mage, Alejandra just wants to see her family in Zobeck again. She is terrified of Vordu and refuses to fight with him.

- **Khadamar, lawful neutral mountain dwarf**. A young adult, Khadamar is Deskorma's brother and noble heir to a small canton in the Ironcrags. He has always preferred human-style diplomacy to traditional dwarven combat and is willing to work with anyone to escape.

- **Deskorma, neutral evil mountain dwarf**. Khadamar's younger sister as well as a seasoned and power-hungry gladiator, Deskorma is next in line for the throne and wants to see her brother fall in the tournament. She wishes for the tournament to go on and aids no escape plans unless she a PC agrees to kill her brother.

- **Vordu, chaotic evil derro**. This wild-eyed, truly insane assassin wants nothing more than to see the darakhul burn. If the PCs help him escape, he buries a dagger in one of their backs as a parting gift. Vordu tries to speak in limericks but isn't very good at it. He sees Temmy as a rat to be kicked around.

- **Temmy, lawful good kobold**. Though a commoner, she is an expert trapsmith, even when using mundane materials in poor conditions. She cheerfully works with anyone but the dwarves; to her, they are almost as bad as the darakhul.

**Calmed Slaves**. Of the 625 slaves in Gonderif, about half of them have undergone a procedure called the Calming. A calmed slave is murdered as cleanly as possible—without damaging muscle or bone—and reanimated as a mindless, obedient undead. Darakhul, generally prefer calmed slaves to living ones, but they are costly to create and decay prohibitively quickly unless properly preserved. The wealthy Duke Radu Kopecs, lord of Gonderif, uses calmed slaves as laborers and janitors for the Undying Tournament. PCs who disguise themselves as darakhul can fool the undead thralls into performing tasks for them.

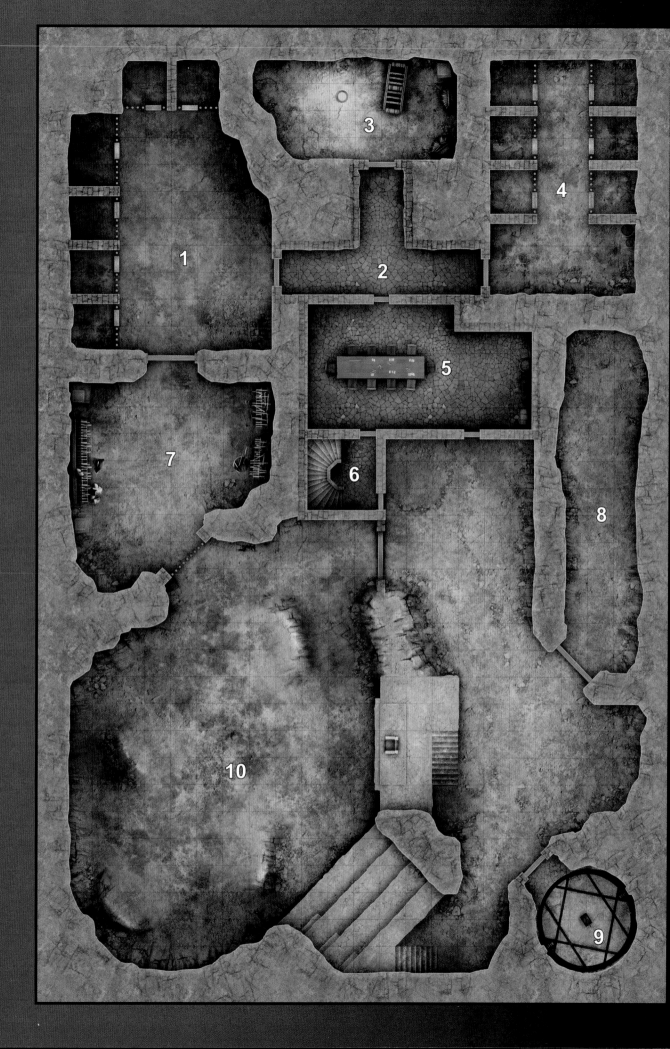

# ADVENTURE HOOKS

As your players' GM, you know best how to involve the PCs in this adventure. The following adventure hooks are provided to inspire and assist you.

- **Escape.** The PCs are captives of the Ghoul Imperium, and have been sentenced to fight to the death in the Undying Tournament. As 8th-level characters, they were likely captured as prisoners of war, either during a darakhul surface raid or when the PCs attacked a darakhul outpost. If you choose this adventure hook, the PCs awaken in chains in Area 1, stripped of their gear (see Area 5).

- **Rescue.** A friend or ally has been captured by the Imperium. The PCs learn through divinations or reconnaissance that their friend has resisted the ghouls at every turn and has been sentenced to fight to the death in the Undying Tournament in Gonderif. The same intelligence that delivered this news also tells of a secret aboveground entrance into the tournament grounds. If you choose this adventure hook, the PCs make their way into the tunnels that lead into Area 10.

- **Revolution.** The Imperium must fall! Striking at Gonderif will cripple its production of weapons and armor, hamstringing the Imperial Legions. With the Corpse Tearer legion protecting the city, a direct assault is ill-advised, but an intelligence report states Duke Radu Kopecs, lord of Gonderif, is attending an event called the Undying Tournament. Assassinating him will likely incite a revolution among the slaves and send the city into chaos. If you choose this adventure hook, the PCs make their way into the tunnels that lead into Area 10.

# ADVENTURE START

All areas within this location are completely dark, unless illuminated by another source.

**Total Party Kill.** If the PCs are all rendered unconscious during an escape attempt, they are not killed outright. Instead, they are returned to their cells. When they awaken (at 1 hit point) they have time to recover before the tournament begins.

**Undying Tournament.** The tournament begins 6 hours after the start of the adventure (if an escape attempt has not been made before then). Three loud blasts of a horn herald the arrival of Duke Radu Kopecs and his retainers as four dozen ghouls spill into the coliseum (Area 10). At this signal, six darakhul (see *Midgard Bestiary*, page 28) enter the PCs' cellblock and usher them into the Staging Area (Area 7), where they are prepared for combat.

The rules of the tournament are explained to them: In the first round, each character is pitted against a wild beast in single combat. In the second round, the survivors fight one-on-one until only half remain. The final round is a free for all, with the last creature standing declared the victor. Magic is not permitted in the tournament, as enforced by each combatant's rare spellbinding shackles (see Area 1).

The ghouls do not reveal everything about their cruel sport to the victims, however. For more information, see Running the Tournament in Area 10.

## 1. SOUTHERN CELL BLOCK

*Slate-gray walls. Cramped, iron-barred cells. The pervasive smell of urine mixed with corpse rot. And an incessant dripping sound from somewhere just out of sight. If you didn't know better, you might think this cell block is one of the Eleven Hells.*

If the PCs were captured by the darakhul before the events of this adventure, they awaken here locked in separate cells without any of their equipment. Their equipment is stored in a chest in Area 5. They are restrained by *rare spellbinding shackles* (see below). Any cells not occupied by PCs contain captive NPCs of the GM's choice (see Factions, above).

Despite being coated in mildew and dried gore, the cells are sturdy, requiring a successful DC 25 Strength or DC 30 Disable Device check to open (each check takes 10 minutes). A patrol of two darakhul (see *Midgard Bestiary*, page 28) from Area 5 passes through this cell block once every two hours, alerting the rest of the guards if the prisoners have escaped either their cells or the block.

**Doors.** Both doors in this room have a complex internal lock, requiring a key held by the Masked Warden (Area 6), or a DC 30 Disable Device check to open.

## SPELLBINDING SHACKLES

**Aura** moderate abjuration; **CL** 11th
**Slot** wrists; **Price** 66,000 gp (rare), 99,000 gp (very rare), 132,000 gp (legendary); **Weight** 2 lbs.

### DESCRIPTION

While bound by these mithral shackles, the wearer cannot cast spells of a certain level or below. The spell level, along with the Strength DC to break the manacles, **Disable Device** DC to pick the lock, or Escape Artist DC to slip out of the manacles is determined by the item's rarity, as shown on the table. The chain binding the manacles can be broken or removed without ending this item's enchantment; only breaking the manacles themselves ends the antimagic effect.

| Rarity | Spell Level | Strength/Disable Device/ Escape Artist DC |
|---|---|---|
| Rare | 3rd or lower | 20 |
| Very Rare | 5th or lower | 25 |
| Legendary | 7th or lower | 30 |

### CONSTRUCTION

**Requirements** Craft Wondrous Item, *antimagic field*;
**Cost** 33,000 gp (rare), 49,500 gp (very rare), 66,000 gp (legendary)

## 2. CROSS HALLS

This hall echoes all hours of the day with screams from the torture chamber to the west, only falling silent when the Undying Tournament is in progress. The otherwise constant noise masks any violence perpetrated here. The eastern and western doors are unlocked, but the northern and southern doors require a successful DC 25 Strength or DC 30 Disable Device check to unlock.

## 3. TORTURE CHAMBER

*This is a room of suffering, filled with implements of torture designed solely to strip a being of its will to live. The screams of one poor prisoner, stretched out on a rack and struck repeatedly by a ghoul's lash, ring through the room. His wails seem to shake the foundation of the room, rattling chains and causing iron maidens to shudder. The three ghouls gleefully torturing this prisoner do not notice your entrance.*

One NPC of the GM's choice (see Factions above) is stretched on a rack, being beaten by three snarling darakhul. Four ghouls hang by thumbscrews in the north of the room—the reanimated remains of fatally tortured prisoners. They tear out the screws and attack when commanded.

**Treasure.** An iron pot filled with liquid gold bubbles over an open fire against the western wall. The gold inside is worth 100 gp.

## 4. NORTHERN CELL BLOCK

*This dingy cell block is cramped and filled with slaves—most of whom are already corpses. One living prisoner glances fearfully at you as you open the door, but her expression changes from fearful to confused when she realizes you aren't ghouls at all!*

The cells in this block are populated by any NPCs the PCs have not yet met (see Factions above). Any empty cells contain the rotting carcasses of the tournament's previous victims. Despite being coated in mildew and dried gore, the cells are sturdy, requiring a successful DC 25 Strength or DC 30 Disable Device check to open (each check takes 10 minutes).

A patrol of two darakhul from Area 5 passes through this cell block once every hour, alerting the rest of the guards if the prisoners have escaped either their cells or the block.

## 5. MONITOR HALL

*This guard post is brimming with armed ghouls. Over a dozen darakhul prison guards are sparring, gambling, and telling gruesome stories, while a handful of other ghouls are keeping the room clean and fetching items for the guards. Several ghouls are sitting around a table in the room; one is scribbling notes inside a hefty ledger.*

If the PCs began as prisoners, read:

*Another ghoul is trying on armor and weapons that have been haphazardly thrown into a rusty chest—your stolen equipment!*

This guard post is the center of Corpse Tearer activity in the slave pit. At any given time, 5 darakhul and 10 ghasts (about half the total garrison) are drilling, sleeping, or killing time here. They see this tournament as a gross excess and would rather be defending Gonderif itself. The other half of the guards are patrolling the grounds, keeping watch in the Sentinel Tower (Area 6), or watching an animal fight in Coliseum (Area 10). If combat erupts here, one ghoul rushes to Area 6 to alert the warden.

The guards here are tended to by a small staff of calmed slaves (see Factions above). These 4 brain-dead ghouls tend to their undead masters' every whim, as long as the commands are simple enough for them to comprehend.

Any slave that has undergone the Calming is conditioned to recognize all undead creatures that wear the Corpse Tearers' uniform as masters.

**Ledger.** A ledger on the table assigns certain slaves to fight certain animals in the first round of the tournament. The list reads:

- Old human – Tiger
- Dwarf male – Giant Boar
- Dwarf female – Elephant
- Derro male – Winter Wolf
- Dragon runt – Lion
- New arrivals – Wyvern

**Treasure.** If the PCs began this adventure as prisoners, then their equipment is stored in a rusty, unlocked chest in a corner of this room. The chest also contains an additional 3,000 gold in tribute given to the legion. A rack of vials and scroll tubes on the table also contains 5 potions of cure serious wounds and 3 scrolls of restoration.

## 6. SENTINEL TOWER

*A winding staircase climbs five stories to the top of this tower, where the pervasive smell of death lingers. Two ghouls look out over the edge of the tower, unaware of you, using large glass lamps to cast beams of ghostly green light into the prison yard. A golden font filled with tiny bones rests on a pedestal in the center of the tower.*

This 50-foot-tall tower has a clear view of everything within the slave pit, save for the inside of the prison itself. A spiraling staircase leading to the top takes up most of the tower; no landings exist between the ground floor and the top. Four will-o'-wisps shimmer at the corners of the tower. Instead of shining light in a radius, the wisps shine a 40-foot-long, 5-foot wide beam of light, with an additional 40 feet of dim light beyond that. These wisps are trapped in enchanted glass and cannot move or attack. The two darakhul atop this tower cannot see beyond 60 feet with their darkvision and must use these searchlights to scan the grounds.

In the center of the tower is a golden font emblazoned with the frightful crest of the Ghoul Imperium. Inside the font is a small heap of tiny bones and platinum-plated teeth. This bone collective (see *Midgard Bestiary*, page 12) is the Masked Warden, the sadistic hive mind behind the Undying Tournament and keeper of the slave pit. She usually exists as a swarm of bones and teeth; she takes singular form only when intruders enter her tower, the alarm is raised, the tournament begins, or she decides to personally torture one of the imprisoned slaves (Area 3). In this singular form, the Warden drapes her humanoid frame in a shadowy cloak and hides behind a bone-white mask.

**Treasure.** The golden font holding the Warden's bones is worth 1,500 gp, and her platinum-plated fangs are worth 100 gp each (3,200 gp total). A single master key rests beneath her remains; this key opens all locks within the complex.

**Levers.** Two levers on the east and west of the tower open the portcullis in Area 7 and the northern door in Area 10, respectively.

## 7. COLISEUM STAGING AREA

*Eerie green light flickers across the walls of this cave, cast by globes of light that dance around the cavern. The walls of the cave are lined with suits of armor and racks of gladiatorial weapons. At the far end, a heavy portcullis bars the passage between you and the coliseum.*

This small cave is wedged between the prison and the coliseum, and it is dimly lit by ghostly *dancing lights*. The light glints ominously on the bare steel of the armor and weapons lining the cave walls. The weapons' handles are caked with dried blood from dozens—if not hundreds—of contestants that died holding them in tournaments past.

**Portcullis.** This portcullis can only be opened by pulling a lever in Area 6. Its bars are wide enough for a Tiny creature to fit through, and it requires a successful DC 25 Climb check to scale.

**Armament.** The selection of weapons and armor here is limited, but not excessively so. All simple weapons can be found here, and there is a 75% chance a specific martial weapon can be found as well. There are twelve sets of nets and tridents, as well as ten gladii (short swords). All forms of light armor can be found here, and there is a 75% chance a specific set of medium armor can be found as well. There is also one set of plate armor.

**Tournament.** If the PCs are brought here to prepare for the Undying Tournament, their darakhul captors do not enter the chamber, but they lock the door behind the PCs. The PCs are the first to arrive, followed by any NPCs who were in their cell block, then NPCs in the Northern Cell Block (Area 4). Whatever resolve those NPCs had falters here, and emotions run high. Vordu the insane derro may try to eliminate the competition early by attempting to murder one of the PCs here. The chains on the characters' spellbinding shackles are removed as they arrive, though the manacles still inhibit spellcasting.

## 8. ANIMAL PENS

*If the foul stench of death weren't enough, this wide pen smells also of decaying animal fur. A strange herd of assorted animals shambles around this enclosure.*

These pens hold juju zombie animals used in the first round of the Undying Tournament.

The zombified animals here include an elephant, a giant boar, a tiger, a lion, a winter wolf, and a wyvern. They hunger only for living flesh and attack any living creatures that enter their pen.

### ZOMBIE BOAR — CR 5

**XP 1,600**
Dire boar juju zombie
NE Large undead
**Init** +5; **Senses** darkvision 60 ft., low-light vision, scent; Perception +9

**DEFENSE**

**AC** 19, touch 10, flat-footed 18 (+1 Dex, +9 natural, −1 size)
**hp** 22 (5d8)
**Fort** +0, **Ref** +2, **Will** +5
**Defensive Abilities** channel resistance +4, ferocity; **DR** 5/magic and slashing; **Immune** cold, electricity, *magic missile*, undead traits; **Resist** fire 10

**OFFENSE**

**Speed** 40 ft.
**Melee** gore +10 (2d6+8), slam +10 (1d8+8)
**Space** 10 ft.; **Reach** 10 ft.

**STATISTICS**

**Str** 27, **Dex** 12, **Con** —, **Int** 2, **Wis** 13, **Cha** 8
**Base Atk** +3; **CMB** +12; **CMD** 23
**Feats** Improved Initiative, Skill Focus (Perception), Toughness
**Skills** Climb +16, Perception +9; **Racial Modifiers** +8 Climb

### ZOMBIE ELEPHANT — CR 8

**XP 4,800**
Elephant juju zombie
NE Huge undead
**Init** +5; **Senses** darkvision 60 ft., low-light vision, scent; Perception +18

**DEFENSE**

**AC** 21, touch 9, flat-footed 20 (+1 Dex, +12 natural, −2 size)
**hp** 38 (11d8−11)
**Fort** +3, **Ref** +4, **Will** +10
**Defensive Abilities** channel resistance +4; **DR** 10/magic and slashing; **Immune** cold, electricity, *magic missile*, undead traits; **Resist** fire 10

**OFFENSE**

**Speed** 40 ft.
**Melee** gore +18 (2d8+12), slam +18 (2d6+12), slam +18 (2d6+12)
**Space** 15 ft.; **Reach** 10 ft.
**Special Attacks** trample (2d8+18, DC 27)

**STATISTICS**

**Str** 34, **Dex** 12, **Con** —, **Int** 2, **Wis** 13, **Cha** 7
**Base Atk** +8; **CMB** +22 (+24 bull rush); **CMD** 33 (35 vs. bull rush, 37 vs. trip)
**Feats** Endurance, Great Fortitude, Improved Bull Rush, Improved InitiativeB, Iron Will, Power Attack, Skill Focus (Perception), ToughnessB
**Skills** Climb +20, Perception +18; **Racial Modifiers** +8 Climb

### ZOMBIE LION — CR 4

**XP 1,200**
Lion juju zombie
NE Large undead
**Init** +8; **Senses** darkvision 60 ft., low-light vision, scent; Perception +6

**DEFENSE**

**AC** 19, touch 13, flat-footed 15 (+4 Dex, +6 natural, −1 size)
**hp** 17 (5d8−5)
**Fort** −1, **Ref** +5, **Will** +5
**Defensive Abilities** channel resistance +4; **DR** 5/magic and slashing; **Immune** cold, electricity, *magic missile*, undead traits; **Resist** fire 10

**OFFENSE**

**Speed** 40 ft.
**Melee** bite +9 (1d8+7 plus grab), 2 claws +9 (1d4+7), slam +9 (1d8+7)
**Space** 10 ft.; **Reach** 5 ft.
**Special Attacks** pounce, rake (2 claws +9, 1d4+7)

**STATISTICS**

**Str** 25, **Dex** 19, **Con** —, **Int** 2, **Wis** 12, **Cha** 6

**Base Atk** +3; **CMB** +11 (+15 grapple); **CMD** 25 (29 vs. trip)

**Feats** Improved Initiative, Run, Skill Focus (Perception), Toughness[B]

**Skills** Acrobatics +9 (+13 to jump), Climb +15, Perception +6, Stealth +6 (+10 in undergrowth); **Racial Modifiers** +4 Acrobatics, +8 Climb, +4 Stealth, +4 Stealth in undergrowth

## ZOMBIE TIGER     CR 5

**XP 1,600**

Tiger juju zombie

NE Large undead

**Init** +7; **Senses** darkvision 60 ft., low-light vision, scent; Perception +5

**DEFENSE**

**AC** 18, touch 12, flat-footed 15 (+3 Dex, +6 natural, −1 size)

**hp** 21 (6d8−6)

**Fort** +0, **Ref** +5, **Will** +6

**Defensive Abilities** channel resistance +4; **DR** 5 and slashing; **Immune** cold, electricity, magic missile, undead traits; **Resist** fire 10

**OFFENSE**

**Speed** 40 ft.

**Melee** bite +11 (2d6+8 plus grab), 2 claws +12 (1d8+8 plus grab), slam +11 (1d8+8)

**Space** 10 ft.; **Reach** 5 ft.

**Special Attacks** pounce, rake (2 claws +12, 1d8+8 plus grab)

**STATISTICS**

**Str** 27, **Dex** 17, **Con** —, **Int** 2, **Wis** 12, **Cha** 6

**Base Atk** +4; **CMB** +13 (+17 grapple); **CMD** 26 (30 vs. trip)

**Feats** Improved Initiative, Skill Focus (Perception), Toughness[B], Weapon Focus (claw)

**Skills** Acrobatics +8 (+12 to jump), Climb +16, Perception +5, Stealth +5 (+9 in areas of tall grass), Swim +10; **Racial Modifiers** +4 Acrobatics, +8 Climb, +4 Stealth, +4 Stealth in areas of tall grass

## ZOMBIE WINTER WOLF     CR 6

**XP 2,400**

Winter wolf juju zombie

NE Large undead (cold)

**Init** +6; **Senses** darkvision 60 ft., low-light vision, scent; Perception +12

**DEFENSE**

**AC** 21, touch 11, flat-footed 19 (+2 Dex, +10 natural, −1 size)

**hp** 33 (6d8+6)

**Fort** +2, **Ref** +4, **Will** +6

**Defensive Abilities** channel resistance +4; **DR** 5/magic and slashing; **Immune** cold, electricity, magic missile, undead traits; **Resist** fire 10

**Weaknesses** vulnerability to fire

**OFFENSE**

**Speed** 50 ft.

**Melee** bite +10 (1d8+7 plus 1d6 cold and trip), slam +10 (1d8+7)

**Space** 10 ft.; **Reach** 5 ft.

**Special Attacks** breath weapon (15 ft. cone, 6d6 cold, Reflex DC 13 for half, usable every 1d4 rounds)

**STATISTICS**

**Str** 24, **Dex** 15, **Con** —, **Int** 9, **Wis** 13, **Cha** 10

**Base Atk** +4; **CMB** +12; **CMD** 24 (28 vs. trip)

**Feats** Improved Initiative, Run, Skill Focus (Perception), Toughness[B]

**Skills** Acrobatics +2 (+10 to jump), Climb +15, Perception +12, Stealth +6 (+12 in snow), Survival +9; **Racial Modifiers** +8 Climb, +2 Perception, +2 Stealth, +6 Stealth in snow, +2 Survival

**Languages** Common, Giant

## ZOMBIE WYVERN     CR 7

**XP 3,200**

Wyvern juju zombie

NE Large undead

**Init** +6; **Senses** darkvision 60 ft., low-light vision, scent; Perception +15

**DEFENSE**

**AC** 23, touch 11, flat-footed 21 (+2 Dex, +12 natural, −1 size)

**hp** 31 (7d8)

**Fort** +1, **Ref** +4, **Will** +8

**Defensive Abilities** channel resistance +4; **DR** 5/magic and slashing; **Immune** cold, electricity, magic missile, undead traits; **Resist** fire 10

**OFFENSE**

**Speed** 20 ft., fly 60 ft. (clumsy)

**Melee** bite +10 (2d6+6 plus grab), slam +10 (1d8+6), sting +10 (1d6+6 plus poison), 2 wings +5 (1d6+3)

**Space** 10 ft.; **Reach** 5 ft.

**Special Attacks** rake (2 claws +10, 1d6+6)

**STATISTICS**

**Str** 23, **Dex** 14, **Con** —, **Int** 7, **Wis** 12, **Cha** 9

**Base Atk** +5; **CMB** +12 (+16 grapple); **CMD** 24

**Feats** Flyby Attack, Improved Initiative, Iron Will, Skill Focus (Perception), Toughness[B]

**Skills** Climb +14, Fly +6, Perception +15, Sense Motive +8, Stealth +5; **Racial Modifiers** +8 Climb, +4 Perception

**Languages** Draconic

**Treasure.** There is no treasure in this pen, but eliminating some or all of the animals in secret before the Undying Tournament may allow some NPCs to survive the first round of the tournament.

## 9. LIFT

*This circular platform is wide enough to hold about ten people in close quarters, and its stone surface has been worn smooth through countless years of use. It is attached by stone gears to tracks running up the length of this shaft.*

The lift is a circular platform connected to an old piece of derro engineering from Gonderif's glory days. Pulling a level on the platform causes it to rapidly ascend towards the city above, reaching the surface in about 30 seconds.

## 10. COLISEUM

**Secret.** A small rocky outcropping in the southeast corner of the arena conceals a secret passageway to the surface, made by the only prisoner ever to escape Gonderif. If the PCs infiltrated the slave pit, they begin inside this tunnel.

*The sand in this wide arena is spattered with dried gore. Gray stone juts out of the sand in places, and the rocky ridge surrounding the arena has been carved into crude benches for spectators.*

If the tournament is in progress, also read:

*On the benches are cheering masses. To the south, a group of ragged, emaciated ghouls scream gleefully; this event may well be the only joy in their wretched existence. To the north, a regal ghoul is dressed in verdant finery, wielding a golden scepter, and holding a golden bowl. He is protected by an armed bodyguard.*

**Running the Tournament.** The Undying Tournament is split into three rounds, with enough time between rounds for the PCs to take a short rest:

In the first round, each PC and NPC faces an undead animal from Area 9 in single combat. The animals faced by the NPCs are described on the ledger in Area 5, with the PCs names left blank. The ledger can be sabotaged, but as written has Alejandra face the tiger, Khadamar the boar, Deskorma the elephant, Vordu the winter wolf, and Temmy the lion. The PCs are to fight against the wyvern together as a special event. Following a battle, all corpses are left in the arena. The NPCs have very little hope of defeating their opponents, but they each have a 10% chance to survive to the tournament's next round.

In the second round, the survivors fight to the death. Try and pair as few PCs against one another as possible; ideally, no more than one pair of PCs must fight each other. All corpses are left in the arena.

In the third round, the remaining combatants fight in a free-for-all. There is a twist, however: after 3 rounds, a wave of necromantic energy sweeps through the arena, reanimating all humanoids who have died so far as ghasts. They attack the nearest living creature.

The last surviving creature is congratulated and then personally slain by Duke Kopecs, "freeing" them from an eternity of undead servitude as promised.

## 10A. DUKE'S SEAT

The highest and best-protected seats are reserved for darakhul nobility, with a special seat reserved for Duke Radu Kopecs, a darakhul noble (a darakhul with the advanced creature template). When the tournament is in session, the duke is flanked by a darakhul bodyguard that

acts as if it is the caster of a shield other spell with the duke as the subject. If the Masked Warden (a bone collective) is still alive, her golden font rests beside the duke. They are tended by four calmed ghouls.

## 10B. BEGGARS' SEATS

Dozens of pathetic beggar ghouls fill the cheap seats. They are an excitable mass and are easily swayed by displays of power. Most of these ghouls are laborers treated barely better than living slaves, and they leap on the opportunity to seize power from the duke if both the Masked Warden and the duke's bodyguard suddenly fall under attack.

# CONCLUSION

The Undying Tournament can be a standalone adventure or the beginning of a high-level war or espionage campaign with the Ghoul Imperium as major villains. NPCs like Alejandra or the dwarf nobles may be powerful allies if the adventurers return to Zobeck or the Ironcrag cantons.

**Continuing the Adventure.** If the PCs did not discover the secret exit out of the slave pit and instead rode the lift into Gonderif, their escape may have only just begun. Consider using the Ghoul Outpost lair from the Book of Lairs to represent their escape from the Corpse Tearer legion through the mining tunnels of Gonderif.